# KATHRYN WOLFE

Kathryn Wolfe is Senior Lecturer in Media Performance and Course Leader in TV Production at the University of Bedfordshire. She has extensive TV directing experience in news, current affairs, children's, magazine and documentary programmes. BBC credits include *Breakfast Time*, *The Clothes Show*, *Crimewatch UK*, *Playschool*, *Jackanory*, *Record Breakers*, *Teletubbies*, and over seventy episodes of *Tweenies*; ITV credits include *Michael Winner's True Crimes*, *Britain's Most Wanted*, *Drivers from Hell*, *One in a Million*, *Strange But True*, *Crime Monthly* and *The Six O'Clock Show*. Kathryn has directed over one hundred educational programmes for Teachers TV.

The dozens of TV presenters Kathryn has worked with include Chris Tarrant, Danny Baker, Emma Freud, Penny Smith, Nick Ross, Selina Scott, Michael Aspel, Paul Ross, Justin Fletcher and Hermione Cockburn. In 2003, Kathryn set up Pukka Presenting to train TV presenters and deliver business presentation skills. Since then she has coached hundreds of TV presenters and launched countless careers.

Kathryn is a regular tutor in adult education and has devised short courses in TV presenting and presentation skills for the City Lit, Actors Centre, Ravensbourne College of Design and Communication, University of Bristol Lifelong Learning Department, University College for the Creative Arts, Academy of Live and Recorded Arts and London College of Communication.

After attending Henrietta Barnett School in London, Kathryn read Drama at Bristol University. Kathryn is an Associate of the Higher Education Academy.

For up-to-date information see www.pukkapresenting.co.uk

# SO YOU WANT·TO BE A TV PRESENTER?

*Discover your
TV-presenting potential
– and launch a new career*

## Kathryn Wolfe

*Foreword by Chris Tarrant*

**NICK HERN BOOKS**
London
www.nickhernbooks.co.uk

A Nick Hern Book

SO YOU WANT TO BE A TV PRESENTER?
first published in Great Britain in 2010
by Nick Hern Books
14 Larden Road, London w3 7st

Cover designed by Peter Bennett
Author photo by Arif Hussein

Typeset by Nick Hern Books, London
Printed and bound in Great Britain by
Ashford Colour Press, Gosport, Hampshire

A CIP catalogue record for this book
is available from the British Library

isbn 978 1 84842 062 5

**Mixed Sources**
Product group from well-managed
forests and other controlled sources
www.fsc.org   Cert no. SGS-COC-003985
© 1996 Forest Stewardship Council
FSC

*For all my family,*
*especially Arif, Omar and Soraya*
*for their patience and support,*
*and Ronnie and Rose*
*for their never-ending help and guidance*

# Contents

# Foreword

I feel like I've been on television for ever. I know what you're thinking – from the state of me, I *look* like I've been on television for ever!

It certainly has been a very long time since I first appeared in front of a TV camera back in 1972 on ATV in Birmingham. I worked on the nightly regional-news programme in the Midlands for years and started doing a little children's show called *Tiswas* at the weekends. So, for seven or eight years it meant I was on television for six or seven days a week, usually live.

And I would absolutely recommend it to anybody. I thoroughly enjoyed it, I've had a great life out of it, I've travelled the world working, and I've been lucky enough to interview just about everybody I ever wanted to meet. When you do it night after night, you almost forget that you're on camera.

But it's amazing how much things have changed. In those early days there was no Autocue. This meant we actually had to learn our links and read the news off a clipboard. I remember the wonders of Autocue when it first arrived – it was pretty basic. The scripts you put into the machine were actually rolls of paper and you could make changes on your own script with a magic marker just seconds before you went on air. There is now a whole new breed of television presenters who have only ever grown up with Autocue. Some handle it very well, some do it in a rather glassy-eyed way, like a rabbit blinking into the headlights, and one or two do it well but haven't got an ad lib in their body.

This splendid book covers every aspect of the job from how to talk to the camera, how to overcome nerves, how to write scripts and even how to choose the right agent. It's all good stuff, particularly important is Kathryn's suggestion that if you need a demo tape you should get a few quid together, any way that you can, and make a really good quality product. If it's low-grade and shoddy, although you personally may be very good, producers will tend to reach for the waste bin and chuck your tape away without giving it more than a cursory glance. Do the best quality tape that you can, send it to absolutely everybody, be prepared for rejection and disappointment, but persevere and pester, pester, pester. There are a huge number of television channels these days and they are increasing all the time. If you have the talent, and the determination you *will* succeed.

Good luck and I look forward to seeing you on my telly!

*Chris Tarrant*

# Introduction

In 2004, after twenty-five years as a TV director, I gave a one-day workshop in TV presenting at the Actors Centre, London. It was called Pukka Presenting, and the class was full to overflowing, with a waiting list – actors were desperate to discover their TV-presenting potential and gain another string to their bow.

Since then I have given TV-presenter training to packed workshops all over the UK, not just attended by actors but by people from all walks of life, from an infinite variety of backgrounds and professions, and of all ages.

In 2006, I was appointed Senior Lecturer in Media Performance at the University of Bedfordshire, a post that has given me the opportunity to teach TV presenting within higher education. The good news is that whether in short courses, further education, adult education or higher education – training works! Students have successfully passed auditions, acquired experience, started presenting, and are getting paid for it!

This book is based on my experiences of tutoring and working with presenters and is intended as a guide to help you approach the world of TV presenting – a practical handbook of training and job-seeking advice. It is packed with tips from presenters who have fresh details of what to expect in screen tests and in the industry, full of success stories, and anecdotes about what you can expect.

Although some of the contributors may be well-known to you, most are not household names (yet!), but they have started the ball rolling and they have newly acquired experiences to pass on. This is the tip of the iceberg – there are thousands of people earning money from presenting, and this book will give you a unique insight into how they got started. If you are considering entering the TV-presenting industry then the quotes from working presenters will be illuminating – a rich source of experience and support to help you, too, enter the profession.

In addition, experts from several areas of TV production have given their words of wisdom and advice on TV presenting, from agents and producers to executive producers and directors, ranging from shopping channels to children's programmes to weather presenting.

This book aims to show you that the world of TV presenting is not a closed shop – in fact, there has never been a better time to enter. With the explosion of TV channels and online platforms, the demand for presenters is still increasing.

You can read answers to frequently asked questions such as 'How do I train as a TV presenter?', 'Do I need an agent?', 'What should I put on my showreel?', 'What happens in TV-presenting auditions?', 'If I don't have any experience, how can I write a presenting CV?' and 'How do I get a presenting job?'

The following chapters will concentrate on the key features of your training, and provide invaluable advice on the practicalities of finding work. You will have to do your bit too! This is a hands-on training manual and you will need to hone your skills. You should practise the exercises to enable you to speak to camera naturally, and you will need to put in the time required to find and apply for presenting jobs.

Included in this book are practical exercises for you to try out at home. Ideally, you should use a video camera to record your work and play it back to check how you are doing. Camcorders can be purchased very reasonably online – you do not need a state-of-the-art model, or even a new one. A second-hand one is fine, or perhaps join forces with some like-minded friends, or borrow one. Some presenters just practise in front of the mirror, which can be very useful, but that has the disadvantage of not giving you a record of your work.

My interests and experience combine industry practice with education and teaching, so I am aiming to give you a set of skills with which you will be able to have fun, earn money, and enhance or even change your existing career.

In the Appendix, you will find checklists, which you can photocopy, to help you assess your progress. These self-evaluation strategies will enable you to continually monitor your development through the practical exercises – but you must be honest with yourself! There is a troubleshooting guide to help you double-check your work, and there are pages of resources to point you on your way. With the skills you can acquire from this book you will learn how to improve your performance; the self-assessment tools will give you the ability to reflect and think about your work – to help you to recognise the good bits and the not-so-good bits!

TV-presenting jobs are usually short contracts or part-time, so you will not necessarily need to give up your day job – the choice is yours!

If you've ever had a dream, ever said to yourself, 'I could present that!', then my advice is to give it a go!

Good luck.

## Before you start

*How to video yourself*

Throughout this book you will find exercises to improve your technique (these are marked with a TV icon ▢). There are also some that are best tried if you them record on video, and then play them back for analysis (these are marked with a camera icon 📹). You will find it very useful to use a camcorder. If you buy one, hopefully it will more than pay for itself in due course, and you can use it for training and development purposes, as well as to shoot your showreel items. The recordings do not have to be broadcast quality, as long as the vision and sound are good enough to see and hear your performances clearly. It is perfectly acceptable to use a camera with a built-in internal microphone; you do not need an external mic.

The majority of the recordings can be made inside your home. Find a suitable room, preferably quiet with ample lighting, and set up the camcorder on a tripod, facing the spot where you will be presenting from. I suggest you should present from a sofa or comfy chair, or seated at a kitchen table, or on a bedroom chair. Make sure the backdrop to the shot is not too distracting – plainer backgrounds without too much clutter are best. Avoid shooting against windows as that can make the picture too much of a silhouette – your facial expressions and features should be visible.

The framing should include your head and shoulders, with the breast pocket at the bottom of the frame. Do not totally fill the frame with just your face; make sure you include the head and neckline with a little extra room at the top and bottom of frame.

To set the framing, sit in the presenter's seat and ask a friend to line up the shot. Or, if you are on your own, frame up the shot as best you can, press record, sit in the presenting seat, talk to the camera, and then play back the test recording to check the image. Test the sound levels too – make sure you are not shouting, just speak naturally.

To view the recordings it is best to play them back through a television or computer screen – the bigger the better! Camcorders usually come with the leads to make these connections. I do not recommend viewing your performances back on the camera viewfinder or flip-out screen, as the image will be too small to make proper judgements.

You can re-record on tapes over and over again, or if you would like to keep the tapes to chart your progress, make each recording on a new section of tape and review them back every now and again to see how your style is developing.

*Basic terms*

This book is, I hope, self-explanatory, and not too technical. However, there may be some terms with which you are unfamiliar, and below are a few definitions. There is a link to a useful glossary of television production terms in the Appendix.

PIECE TO CAMERA   When the presenter talks directly to camera.

AD LIB   When the presenter does not have an actual script, but creates the script off-the-cuff as he or she speaks to camera.

PROMPT   A device which scrolls the script in front of the camera lens for the presenter to read, yet the viewer cannot see the words. Most commonly used prompting systems are Autocue, Autoscript and Portaprompt.

IN-EAR TALKBACK   An earpiece worn by presenters which enables them to receive instructions.

# PART ONE

# Why?

## Why now?

**66** As I got older I went on to pursue a more sensible occupation as an administrator and now at twenty-nine and knowing myself more, I felt it was time to do something I really wanted to do and pursue my dreams.

Charmaine Line, presenter, local-news.tv

So you want to be a TV presenter? It's a growing market and there's never been a better time to enter the industry. In recent years we have seen a huge expansion in the number of broadcast programmes and opportunities for presenters on digital TV, internet channels, web videos and other media.

TV channels are developing so quickly that current figures are hard to pin down, but the statistics speak for themselves: in 1982 there were still only three TV channels, BBC1, BBC2 and ITV. In October 2009, according to Ofcom, there were 831 cable and satellite services available in the UK.

You can find a channel for almost every niche and genre from education (Teachers TV) to paranormal (Psychic TV), online jewellery (Gemondo TV) to Asian entertainment (AAG TV), religion (Gospel Channel) to football (Liverpool FC TV), finance (Bloomberg Television) to lifestyle (Horse and Country TV) – and presenting for the less mainstream channels is a popular and more approachable route into the business. These three presenters are typical of those who have entered the industry via the lesser-known channels:

**66** I went part time at work to give me more time to pursue presenting. I took a big pay cut but it has definitely been worth it. Presenting is my passion and I feel like I actually have a balanced life now, as opposed to trying to squeeze everything into evenings, weekends and days off.

> Cate Conway, presenter, *The Seven Thirty Show* (UTV),
> *Cooking in the Community* (Northern Visions)

**66** I have always enjoyed performing – or being the 'front man' – having spent many years acting, dancing and singing. I have a passion for the performing arts and I saw TV presenting as an extension of that. I wanted to combine my work experience with my performing skills. I enjoy the TV world and being in a position to entertain or inform an audience. I take bizarre pleasure in putting myself in pressured situations, having to think on my feet or deliver in a live environment. It also offers the opportunity to meet people from all walks of life.

> Howard Corlett, winner, *Sky Search for a Presenter*, 2006;
> presenter, *The Seven Wonders of the Weald* (Sky)

**66** Presenting is an exciting, diverse and flexible profession. You never know where your next project is going to take you.

> Nicci Brighten, presenter,
> *Love Your Home Show*, 2008, Radio Wey 87.9 FM

There are hundreds of channels that could be described as 'minority', but that is the way television is heading: it has become a hugely fragmented market. Whether you are presenting on a mainstream or a smaller channel, your work is still classified as a professional engagement and you gain a screen credit – it does not matter if the audience figures are high or relatively low. In some ways it is actually better to start off presenting on the smaller channels, so as to gain experience before you launch yourself on the mainstream ones.

TV presenting is also more accessible now than it used to be, with more opportunities for different kinds of presenters. In the past, presenters traditionally came from a journalistic or performance background, whereas nowadays if you have the right personality and some training you can look for a TV-presenting job to suit your individual interests and hobbies.

It's never been easier to enter the industry, especially if you have access to the internet. You will find dozens of TV-presenter auditions advertised online, sites where you can seek work, upload your own video material, advertise your skills and experience, and organise your career. Showreel footage will be necessary for some job applications, but not all.

There are plenty of presenter training courses available, ranging from one day to one year. Some courses include showreels, and some don't, but as the equipment needed to make showreels has become cheaper and more compact, many presenters make their own reels – or at least one to start them off. It is possible to shoot and edit showreel pieces without going to professional studios and edit facilities, and you can apply for auditions with your homemade reel. I know hundreds of TV presenters who have started this way, even one who waited for her husband to leave the house, set up the camera herself in the kitchen, recorded a cookery item and sent it off for a screen test – she was successful!

For a few pounds each year you can set up your own website to market yourself and stream your items; alternatively, use an existing free site such as YouTube to play out your material. If you can't find a channel to suit your passions and interests you can even set up your own, like Karen Ridgers, who set up veggievision.tv, an internet TV channel for vegetarians.

66 People have always said with my natural and bubbly personality I should be a TV presenter. I love meeting people, talking with them and seem to have a natural ability to help the interviewee feel at ease. It's great fun!

Karin Ridgers, founder/presenter, veggievision.tv

As well as training, you will need some good-quality photos of yourself, a presenting CV, the ability to write a good job application and plenty of enthusiasm. This is what some presenters have said about why they wanted to try presenting:

**66** I like the idea of learning new things every day and having to speak eloquently about a wide range of subjects. The interactive human aspect of presenting and interviewing also really appeals to me.

Hannah McLean, commentator,
*FINA World Swimming Championships*, 2008

**66** I feel that all the skills I have learnt in various jobs through the years will hopefully come together in my presenting. Experience in front of the camera as an actress and time as production assistant and PA will, I hope, lead to a greater understanding of the production process and the importance of teamwork and, of course, communication. Also, I would love to communicate my enthusiasm for property and interiors to a wider audience.

Charlie Lemmer, presenter,
Real Estate Channel, Dubai Eye, Abu Dhabi TV, Current TV

What about you? Are there reasons why you would like to try TV presenting? If so, what are you waiting for?

## Why me?

**66** Competing as an elite athlete has instilled a drive in me to produce the perfect performance whatever that may be. TV presenting is about preparation, and pulling off a polished performance no matter what factors you have to deal with.

Hannah McLean, commentator,
*FINA World Swimming Championships*, 2008 (Bronze Medallist 200m backstroke, 2006 Commonwealth Games)

Why not you? Presenters are only human – they come in all shapes and sizes, an infinite variety of colours, ages, backgrounds and physical types. Each potential presenter is unique with their own set of experiences, skills, qualifications, interests, passions and goals. These are some of the people I've come across at presenting workshops: student, graduate, TV extra, college manager, property investor, interiors consultant, receptionist, air steward, overseas holiday rep, entertainer, retired secretary, retail manager, banker, film reviewer, telephone sales operator, TV researcher, waiter, financial consultant, hedge-fund manager, university lecturer, belly dancer, opera singer, plumber, scientist, healthcare worker, teacher, musician, actor, DIY expert, garden designer, ballroom dancer, Commonwealth rifle shot, trampoline instructor, wine expert, children's author, computer programmer, ice-hockey player, lawyer, civil servant, housewife, artist, vegetarian, catwalk model, Olympic swimmer, shop assistant, dental receptionist, beauty therapist, professional cricketer, journalist, runner-up Miss World, broadcaster, radio producer, art historian, synchronised swimmer, voice-over artist, chef, sales assistant, marketing and PR manager, engineer, IT consultant, hospital ward manager, gospel singer, screenplay writer, bus driver, travel agent, jazz singer, international triathlete.

To become a presenter you do not need actual qualifications, there are no prerequisites or accreditations. Literally anyone from any walk of life can become a TV presenter – what matters is that you are able to engage with the camera, connect to the viewer, have something to say and know how to say it. Even if you receive a certificate to prove you have completed a presenter-training course, in order to gain employment you will need to succeed in auditions, screen tests or interviews, and show that you can do the job.

Some presenters have taken the plunge and given up their former careers:

**❝**I gave up a 'proper' job in the corporate world. Having worked for years in travel I thought I would be ideal for *Wish You Were Here* and the *Holiday Programme*, only to find it was the end of an era for these types of travel formats. It was still worth it… following my heart, my passion and my dream.

Howard Corlett, winner, *Sky Search for a Presenter*, 2006;
presenter, *The Seven Wonders of the Weald* (Sky);
(and former overseas holiday rep, purchasing/product
manager for tour operators, entertainer, ballroom dancer)

Jill Kenton, presenter for jnetradio.com, Hayes FM, QVC, *Dress My Mate*, and contributor to *BBC Breakfast*, was formerly marketing director at bespoke lingerie company Rigby & Peller. Denise Ching, guest presenter of Italian jewellery for QVC, was previously BA cabin crew, and Louise Houghton, presenter for sit-up channels and *SuperCasino*, was a TV production assistant when she was given the chance to present.

I taught a varied mix of people in one 'presenting for beginners' workshop, ranging from a bus driver to a Cambridge graduate: the former was better at presenting than the latter because the bus driver had more confidence and personality. So, do not feel that your background may not be suitable or appropriate – if you can develop the confidence to talk to camera, then you should be able to present.

## Why presenting?

**❝**I work as an entertainer, a circus performer, workshop leader and costume maker. I enjoy the freedom that being freelance gives me, I find fitting all types of work together reasonably straightforward. I have not had a contract longer than two months in the last few years, but have had plenty of work, so at the moment the presenting fits in the same way.

Fiona Watkins, presenter,
Holmwood's English Listening Training

If you are tempted to try presenting, but not sure how it will turn out, you do not have to give up your day job! The way to approach presenting, at first, is to think of it as another string to your bow. You could aim to get experience as a presenter and hopefully start to earn money from it without necessarily changing your career.

TV-presenting jobs are mostly freelance engagements, for varying lengths of time. A contract could range from a few hours to a few days; if you are lucky it could last a few weeks, months or years! As a shopping-channel expert you might be used for years, but your on-screen presenting might only take place for a few hours at a time, with a gap of many months in between.

On the other hand, some presenting jobs can be more full time. A presenter on a daily show or series could be employed for a few days per week for several months or even years. If you are offered this kind of contract, then you may have to put other jobs on hold, or leave your previous employment in order to be available for shoots.

Some people combine presenting with acting, but it can sit alongside many different careers as part of your portfolio of skills.

**"** I am currently running my TV presenting alongside my property and interiors work, as I feel they complement each other: my expertise in property and interiors lends to my skills as a presenter. If the opportunity arose to present full time, though, I would definitely take it.

Charlie Lemmer, presenter,
Real Estate Channel, Dubai Eye, Abu Dhabi TV, Current TV

Lisa Francesca Nand finds her broadcasting, writing, radio and television appearances all feed into one another:

**"** Training as a broadcast journalist rather than solely being a presenter has opened several more doors for me. Having a national radio profile helped me get published in the *Media*

*Guardian* and the *Independent*, and once I had those on my writing CV, other bits and pieces came a bit easier. I am now totally freelance, and at the moment as well as creating and presenting my own travel programmes, I am a freelance writer on travel, health and other subjects. I love the freedom of not having to go to an office every day and never being in a routine. I also do a lot of voice-over work and have had some regular radio slots. Although these various freelance roles are not all about presenting to camera, they do all involve using my journalistic skills and are all under the umbrella of broadcasting. It has also meant that I now realise that doing a bit of writing, a bit of television and a bit of radio is where I would always like to be in terms of a career – an all-round broadcaster rather than solely a presenter.

Lisa Francesca Nand, presenter, talkSPORT radio, Sky Travel; guest presenter, *Sky News*; journalist

Perhaps it's time to discover what you have to offer and what you need to do to get started.

# PART TWO

# What?

## What makes a good TV presenter?

**❝** I think that an important quality for a successful presenter to possess is to be genuine. Your audience are wise to fakes and if you are, they will see it. It's also hard to maintain and 'act' as a presenter, it's so much easier to just be yourself. You definitely need to be able to cope with and stay calm under pressure and be able to think on your feet! I do not think that appearance has a lot to do with someone being a good presenter, I think that a person's personality is always what shines on the screen!

Gemma Hunt, presenter, *Barney's Barrier Reef*, *Xchange* (CBBC); guest co-presenter, *Smile*

In my TV-presenting classes, I ask students what qualities and skills they feel a TV presenter should possess. These are some of the most common answers and descriptions they have suggested:

- To connect with the viewer
- To be endearing
- To be 'in the moment'
- To think on your feet
- To ad lib
- To look trustworthy
- To have clear communication
- To know the subject
- To be 'normal'
- To speak as if to one person
- To be warm

- To be relaxed
- To look happy
- To put the guest at their ease
- To be aware of any irritating habits
- To have energy
- To be confident
- To be articulate
- To be yourself
- To have a 'personality'
- To be friendly
- To have an affinity with the camera
- To cope with disasters
- To have 'style'
- To have good personal grooming

Can you think of any others? Working presenters agree that there are a range of skills and qualities required to do the job effectively.

66 Teamwork and the ability to speak naturally. A great deal of patience is needed, not least because you need to wait for crews to set up. You might do the performance of your life, but if a gel falls out of a light, a battery goes flat or a fly gets into the studio, then you'll need to do it all over again as a first take!

Matthew Tosh, presenter, Teachers TV; guest presenter, *Ministry of Mayhem* (ITV), *Brainiac Live: Test Tube Baby* (Sky)

Very often, people unfamiliar with the role of presenting underestimate the sheer hard work involved in writing, creating, memorising and delivering programme material. I think the necessary qualities fall into five different categories:

1   PERFORMANCE-BASED SKILLS

2   JOURNALISTIC SKILLS AND EDITORIAL JUDGEMENT

3   TECHNICAL ABILITY

4 PERSONALITY

5 PHYSICAL APPEARANCE

Let's start with:

1 PERFORMANCE-BASED SKILLS

Being able to perform for the camera is an essential part of TV presenting. This includes being natural, relaxed and confident, with a warm, open face, an easy voice, good posture, clear diction and good communication skills.

**66** You need to be at ease with yourself, and comfortable with who you are. Otherwise you won't be able to put interviewees or viewers at ease. You need to be happy and full of life...

Cate Conway, presenter, *The Seven Thirty Show* (UTV),
*Cooking in the Community* (Northern Visions)

**66** To be natural and warm in front of the camera, always keeping it real and being yourself, is the key.

Denise Ching, guest presenter, QVC

If you can talk to the camera and relate well to the audience you will be employable, but possibly in a limited capacity; for example, simply reading from a script written by someone else.

2 JOURNALISTIC SKILLS AND EDITORIAL JUDGEMENT

The importance of having a 'journalistic brain' or journalism training cannot be overlooked or overemphasised. Presenters frequently need to structure their own material, editing it in their mind as they speak. Editorial judgement will be employed when researching and writing scripts; improving or rewriting supplied material; generating programme ideas and contributing to the production process; preparing interviews; listening to a guest; controlling and shaping the interview; making sense when ad libbing (using non-scripted material); speaking with a good vocabulary and without repetition; understanding concepts and issues and conveying key themes to the viewer; interpreting briefs and making them 'user-friendly'; and being aware of legal pitfalls when presenting on live TV. Journalism training is not a prerequisite for presenting, but it does open doors and can give you the edge. Becky Jago studied Radio Journalism as part of her undergraduate degree in Media Performance, which helped her to gain presenting/reporting jobs in news:

**❝** To be a newsreader you have to show that you have empathy for the people you are talking about in a story, but somehow stay impartial. It's also very important to be believable, clear and have a certain amount of gravitas! I think the best presenters are those that make it look easy – those that the viewer feels comfortable watching.

Becky Jago, presenter, *Anglia Tonight*, *Newsround*, *Sky Sports News*, GMTV's *Entertainment Today*

## 3 TECHNICAL ABILITY

TV is a technical medium. Although you can record material and load it on the web yourself, if you are involved in traditional TV production, mainstream programmes or sophisticated recording, you will be working with crew in a technical environment. So it is important to have an awareness of what is required from a presenter in these circumstances. By 'technical skills' I do not mean that you need to know how to expose the shot or set up stereo sound, but you should be aware of what the technical team is doing, and why, and more importantly what they expect from you.

Technical skills include understanding camera descriptions such as wide shot, medium close-up, close-up, pan, track, zoom, and how that affects the framing, e.g. whether the shot includes your feet, or your hands. You should know how to walk and talk, sit and stand, hit a mark, handle props, talk to time, maintain continuity, and cope with in-ear talkback, single camera or multi-camera, live or recorded, on location or in studios.

**66** Using talkback well – being able to cope with voices in your head – is a hard task so it probably helps if you're slightly mad!

Charlie Lemmer, presenter,
Real Estate Channel, Dubai Eye, Abu Dhabi TV, Current TV

If you are unfamiliar with any of these terms they are all discussed in the following chapters.

## 4 PERSONALITY

Performance, journalistic and technical skills can largely be taught, practised and acquired through experience, but it will be hard to make a success of presenting if you do not have the right personality to get into the industry and stay in it. TV presenting is a highly competitive business, and you will need the right attributes to survive. Do you get on well with people? Work well in a team? Learn from your mistakes? Are you willing to take direction from others?

To succeed you should assess your personality and evaluate whether you are: popular, endearing, happy, adaptable, good at time management, able to work independently, willing to listen to others, able to get on with the job without distraction, able to be professional at all times, capable of making quick decisions, be a team player, reliable, patient, motivated, willing to take risks, able to take on board new ideas, creative, calm under pressure.

**66** I think presenters need to have the ability to be calm in a high-stress environment and allow their personality to show through whilst being clear and professional. Above all, presenters need to be committed and hard working, as broadcasting is a very competitive industry.

Hannah McLean, commentator,
*FINA World Swimming Championships*, 2008

Be honest with your self-assessment, and try to identify any weaknesses you may have, or traits you would like to improve. You could ask your friends for truthful feedback, take a personality test, or try to change some undesirable habits – if you have any! Some producers will avoid working with presenters who are 'difficult', even if the presenter is more than capable of doing the job. After all, TV production should be fun!

5   PHYSICAL APPEARANCE

And finally, what do you look like? Will the viewer want to turn on the television or computer in the morning and look at you!? When they return from a hard day at work, wanting to relax and be entertained, will they be inspired by your image? On larger-budget productions there might be hair and make-up artists, and even costume designers (more usual for actors than presenters). However, on most TV productions that use presenters, you will be in charge of your own wardrobe.

Pay attention to your physical appearance and personal grooming, make the best of your clothes, accessories and hair. Do you need a new haircut or colour? Would you be proud of your hands if seen in close-up? Do your teeth need whitening? Ladies – do you need a make-up makeover? Gents – do you need a shave or a new jacket? Do your nasal hairs need trimming, or are your eyebrows too bushy? Obviously your appearance does depend on the programme and the context – whether you are presenting from Mount Everest or on the red carpet!

Nigel Dacre, Chief Executive of Inclusive Digital TV, has worked with some of our most famous ITV and ITN newscasters, including Trevor McDonald, Mark Austin, John Suchet, Dermot Murnaghan, Mary Nightingale, Kirsty Young, Nicholas Owen, Katie Derham, Alastair Stewart, Alastair Burnet, Julia Somerville and Carol Barnes:

**66** The internet and the increase in the number of digital channels have in many ways demystified the world of presenting. It's certainly easier to become a presenter than ever before, and many programmes are less formal or 'produced' than they used to be. But I would still argue that the skills required to be a successful presenter have stayed the same – hard work, an ability to deal with the unexpected in live situations, and an on-screen 'presence'. So I would say: new opportunities, but old skills.

Nigel Dacre, formerly Chief Executive of Teachers TV;
Managing Director of Ten Alps Digital;
Editor of *ITV News* (1995–2002)

What are the *old* skills? The aim of this book is to help you learn these skills and enable you to develop them for employment.

## What are the differences between presenting and acting?

**66** Presenting is all about you and your personality in front of the camera drawing in the audience, whereas acting is about being a different person and allowing that character to engage with the audience.

Lesley-Anne Webb, presenter,
Ravensbourne College in-house training courses

Many actors present, but presenting is not acting – or is it? What are the differences? Presenting is about being you – you are not 'in character, playing a role'. Presenters must look at the camera, right into the lens, which for actors is totally against the rules (unless delivering a speech directly to the viewer). So actors must undo all their screen training – delete 'Create a character and never look at the camera', and replace it with 'Be yourself and look straight into the lens.'

66 As a presenter, you always involve the camera, whereas it's only in very specific TV/film roles that an actor would break the illusion and look into the camera. Normally it's a capital offence!

Howard Corlett, winner, *Sky Search for a Presenter*, 2006; presenter, *The Seven Wonders of the Weald* (Sky)

A stage actor has to be seen and heard throughout the auditorium; they are trained to create performances which can be seen from a distance, and develop voices which project to fill huge spaces. Unfortunately, if these larger-than-life facial expressions and booming voices are transferred to a TV programme the effect is 'over the top' and can be comical.

Typically, TV shots of presenters are framed to include head and shoulders, or waist upwards; sometimes the presenter's face almost fills the screen. Sensitive microphones are placed on the lapel or neckline, on a desk where the presenter is sitting or just out of vision, which means that every breath might be picked up by the sound recordist. If the face and voice are clearly visible and audible, then the presenter really shouldn't have to try very hard. Actors often need to retrain their performance for the television screen, to develop a conversational style with the viewer, otherwise their presenting may look artificial and will lack the intimate quality needed to create a bond between presenter and viewer. My advice to actors is: don't reach out to the audience, let the audience find you.

TV has a much faster turnaround than actors may be used to in the theatre, although actors who have been in long-running TV series or 'soaps' will be familiar with working at the speed that TV demands. Rehearsals for stage work can take place over several weeks, whereas rehearsals for television presenters tend to take place on the day of recording/transmission. In theatre work the actor may be given weeks or even months to research their character, but for TV presenting the character is you! Even so, preparation is still vital and could include researching programme content, formulating interview questions, writing scripts, and viewing pre-recorded material.

Whereas in the theatre an actor may have weeks to learn a script, in television it may be days, hours or minutes! But, while the actor may need to repeat the same performance over many weeks, months or even years in the case of long-running shows, the TV presenter only needs to deliver the script to camera until a good take is recorded, or until the live transmission is over, then the script can be literally thrown away. No need to repeat it every night, and twice on matinee days!

**66** In presenting, you are being 'yourself' – or the TV version of you. In acting, you embody someone else and present a character. Acting is more controlled. You have a rigid script and movements to stick to. For presenting you need to be more flexible and more willing to expose yourself.

Cate Conway, presenter, *The Seven Thirty Show* (UTV),
*Cooking in the Community* (Northern Visions)

## What are the similarities between presenting and acting?

There is a lot of common ground between the two – the need to reach an audience, to engage the viewer, whether from a stage or through a camera. In both areas the performer is 'on show'. Even though TV presenters are being themselves, they are still putting on a bit of a performance, a heightened version of themselves, concealing any inner anxieties or off-screen concerns.

Performance techniques are important in both occupations – awareness of body language, posture, correct breathing, effective use of voice, good diction, the right amount of energy, the ability to convey information clearly, the skill of understanding scripts and knowing the importance of appropriate costume and make-up.

As with acting, sincerity is paramount when presenting to camera. Bear in mind that your thoughts, feelings and expressions can be exposed, recorded, replayed and scrutinised. The camera sees everything and transmits it to the viewer. The lens will reveal any insincerities in delivery, tension in the face, and whether there is anything 'behind the eyes' or not. So the level of concentration is always important, and you will need to believe what you are saying.

When it comes to TV acting, actors will be aware that, for screen performances, 'hitting a mark', or moving to a particular spot on the set, can be crucial; it affects whether you are in the light, in focus and audible. The TV-drama director may ask the camera operator to frame up on a close shot of the actor by the downstage coffee table. The exact point will be marked out of shot with tape on the floor and the actor will be expected to hit the mark; if they miss the mark they might be out of focus or poorly framed. In TV drama, where personal mics are rarely used, if you drift from the expected position the sound department may not be able to reach you without the microphone coming into the shot.

The same level of accuracy is required for TV presenters. Sometimes the positions for television need to be very precise to create an attractive framing for the camera. When delivering a piece to camera you may be asked to put your weight on your right foot or your left – as the slight shift in balance can make the difference between an attractive shot of you in front of a village church, or a badly framed shot with the church spire apparently growing out of your head.

When co-presenting with another presenter or interviewing someone else, the floor manager might physically move your chairs or your marks closer together than feels normal in 'real life'. In television, the spaces between people can often look greater than they really are, especially if wide-angle lenses are used that make objects seem further apart, so although it may feel as if you are positioned unnaturally close to the other person, when viewed through the camera it will look totally acceptable.

Many actors have revealed that they find it liberating to present, and they love the responsibility of creating scripts and production content.

66 The main difference that I have found is the importance of the presenter connecting with an audience. I really enjoy the challenges that presenting brings as you no longer have a character to hide behind.

Sam Kidd, presenter, *Hey, Let's Talk* (Sky)

## What is 'being you'?

66 The best presenters are the ones who are just simply themselves!

Rita Sedani, presenter, AAG TV

TV presenting is about 'being you'. It's all about your own personality, and having the confidence to be yourself. If a programme does not go according to plan, or there is a crisis or disaster while on air, you may have to ad lib and keep presenting, hopefully without the viewer knowing anything has gone wrong behind the scenes. If you are playing a part, you may not be able to sustain the performance. But when you are 'being you', or even a slightly enhanced version of you, then coping with disasters and working without a script will be more sincere because you are being yourself.

66 It sounds simple but you have to relax and be yourself, otherwise if you try and put on an act it's hard to sustain it for the camera and you put extra pressure on yourself.

Naomi Evans, presenter,
Ravensbourne College in-house training courses

When you attend a TV-presenting audition the producer/ director will probably assess your personality, your image and whether you are suitable for the job within the first thirty seconds. Of course, it is important that you can do the tasks required, whether it's talking to time or inter- viewing, but a major part of the selection process is also your style and whether your 'face fits'. A presenter is not just the programme host – the presenter represents the pro- gramme, the channel and the branding.

At an acting audition for a stage production, the casting director, producer and director might well be thinking that the actor could be right for the part after some rehearsal, and with the aid of a wig, a costume and make-up. The actor might have several weeks to prepare for the role, to research the background of the play and the character, and to take part in script readings, improvisations, directed rehearsals, run-throughs, technical rehearsals, dress runs, before finally giving a performance in front of an audience.

TV, though, is a fast-turnaround medium. Production schedules require that rehearsing and shooting take place very quickly. There will not be a rehearsal period; instead, just before the actual 'take', there will be a rehearsal of the presenter pieces to camera, which is more of a technical check for camera and sound. Very rarely a presenter may be given some notes from the director, such as to speak more slowly or with more pace – and a line may get rewritten, but on the whole a presenter is chosen because they are right for the show, and after that selection their performance is rarely criticised, and they are unlikely to receive feedback.

The decision to use a particular presenter will be based on what they have done in the past, and on who they are, because there is no lengthy rehearsal process available to allow a presenter to develop and grow into the role. So, be you, and go for the presenting jobs that you feel comfort- able with. If presenting is 'being you', you need to decide who you are!

**❝** It may sound like the ultimate cliché, but the best way to achieve a natural presenting performance is to 'be yourself'. But to be yourself you first need to know who you are and feel comfortable in your own skin. I swear by the mantra: 'Know yourself, Love yourself, Be yourself.'

Nicci Brighten, presenter,
*Love Your Home Show*, 2008, Radio Wey 87.9 FM

What kind of presenter are you? What genre, what channel would you fit into best? Try to identify what areas suit you. Do you see yourself as a daytime chat-show host, or children's presenter? Are you an investigative journalist or shopping-channel guest? Are you a niche digital-channel presenter on highly specialised programmes, or a general sports presenter on a mainstream channel? And how do you find out which areas suit you best?

You may already know the answer. If you are crazy about computers, geeky about gadgets, wild about wildlife or potty about pets, you may have decided what kind of programmes you want to work on. For many presenters it is a dilemma – they worry about which area they are right for, and are unsure where to market themselves. My advice is, if you cannot decide which way to go, try all the avenues and see which doors open – don't pigeon-hole yourself.

Look in the mirror – *objectively* – what do you see? Try to see yourself as others see you. Before you even say a word, what kind of presenting image do you give out? Look on TV – which programmes do you enjoy watching, what subjects are you able to talk about? As you go through the presenter-training exercises in this book, try writing scripted material for different types of programmes. See which ones you feel at home with. Do not draw a line in the sand at this point. For example, if you cannot decide between children's and travel, then try for both. You may need to have more than one showreel and CV, but test the market and see what feedback you get from auditions.

I know a presenter who was torn between sports and entertainment, because she loved football and music – yet she is now happily presenting on a shopping channel as that's the audition that had a successful outcome. Of course, some presenters work for more than one channel, and switch genres, moving from one kind of programming to another. I saw one presenter on two different digital channels on the same day – a travel channel and a shopping channel. This is perfectly acceptable for a freelancer: in a sense, both channels are about selling. Hard current affairs and children's programming would be a tricky combination, so do think about how others will perceive your interests!

66 Don't try to present like someone else. Be yourself. Take aspects of people you admire, of course, but no one wants to see an imitation of someone else who is most likely better than you anyway.

Luke Tudball, presenter,
Ravensbourne College in-house training courses

Before you decide on the area which suits your interests, passions, hobbies and qualifications, you will need to learn the skills and techniques of TV presenting, starting with overcoming nerves.

## What if you get nervous?

66 Checklisting mentally the sequence of what I have to do when cued to start, and then interacting normally with people on set to maintain a normal atmosphere. If that's not possible I breathe and dream of the beach.

Renée Castle, presenter, Caribbean New Media Group,
Caribbean Communications Network,
Sun Community Television

Speaking to a camera, being you, and coping with the technicalities – it can all be a bit nerve-racking. That's to be expected – after all, it's not something most people do every day. TV presenting is a learned skill, and most of us need some basic training, but until you have acquired the training you may find presenting to camera makes you nervous.

A touch of nerves can be a good thing – it helps to give a 'performance'. But when the nerves get the better of you, then the body's normal physiological changes take over, and you can be the victim of foggy brain, dry mouth, knocking knees, palpitations or sweaty palms! Don't panic – it's the adrenaline pumping around your body, and it is a perfectly natural response. It is nature's way of coping with being in an uncomfortable situation, known as 'fight or flight' syndrome, as your body prepares to encounter danger or flee from it.

Your breathing could become fast and shallow, your heart rate could increase, which makes you short of breath, and the result is that your brain doesn't get enough oxygen – not great for remembering scripts! You may also find that you speak too quickly because you are not in control! The dry mouth, knocking knees and sweaty palms are all part of the same condition – a perfectly normal response if you are out of your comfort zone. Not everybody suffers from all the above symptoms, but you may recognise some of them to a greater or lesser extent.

The good news is that you can control the nerves, rather than them controlling you – partly by making physical changes, and partly by rehearsal. What you are aiming for is a little bit of adrenaline, just enough to give you the energy needed for a 'performance'. How much is enough? As a rough guide, if we look at a sliding scale from ten to zero, where ten is totally frozen with fear and zero is completely laid back, you should be somewhere between one and five. Any more than five and you may start to look tense in the face.

Whether you are a company director or a student, you will be used to doing certain tasks frequently, such as making high-level financial decisions, sitting exams or writing reports to a deadline. However, the chances are that the more you do those tasks the more confidently you will approach them.

Exactly the same applies to presenting. TV presenting can make you nervous – until you get used to it. The problem is that not many of us do it frequently, so when asked to present, the situation can become stressful. The answer is to keep practising and take up as many presenting opportunities as possible. A student once told me that she had been too nervous to speak in church and had declined the invitation. Once she had received presenter training she made up her mind that she would ask to deliver a talk in church. Avoidance keeps the problem alive, but by confronting your fears you will overcome them. So, the more you practise the easier it gets.

How exactly can you control the nerves?

**❝**I find a quiet space, away from everyone, about forty minutes before live transmission, and play a few tracks on my iPod. With ten to fifteen minutes to go I check over the running order and chat with guests or the audience to put them at their ease; both of these actions give me a degree of confidence and reassurance that I'm prepared and am on top of things, and that really helps.

Michael O'Donoghue, Higher Education producer/manager;
presenter, Distance Learning TV

**❝**I read the script, read my notes, go over any problematic questions or topics, and then try to find a quirky aside or something to have in my back pocket in case of emergencies!

Luke Tudball, presenter,
Ravensbourne College in-house training courses

You can control anxiety by 'correct' breathing, and to breathe correctly you need to be in a relaxed state. Before looking at how to relax, you need to be aware of posture.

These techniques and principles are all interconnected: good posture aids breathing, good breathing creates relaxation, but over-relaxation leads to poor posture, which hinders breathing. Let's start by looking at posture.

## What is good posture?

In everyday life most of us probably do not give much thought to our posture, but actors, dancers, singers, gymnasts, athletes, musicians, models, people in the public eye and many others will be aware of the difference that good posture can make to their performance. For presenters, a good posture will help your breathing, voice production, and give you authority. By aligning your body in the correct way you will be able to breathe deeply, speak with less effort, and even seem to acquire the air of being an 'expert'. The way you enter a room, shake hands, stand, walk and sit – your posture gives out visual signals about your confidence, well-being and energy, and affects the way you are perceived, both on and off camera.

By good posture I do not mean standing up stiffly with shoulders back and chin in the air. It is more about correct alignment, defying gravity, and using your muscles properly to prevent fatigue, strain, and backache. As a presenter, if you stand or sit erect, with broad shoulders and your head at the right angle you can address the camera and the viewer directly with an elegant and confident poise.

Your posture is all part of your body language – visual signals that can be picked up by the viewer and interpreted in positive or negative ways. This does not just apply to TV presenting, it is something that transfers to everyday communication, and is equally important to remember in business meetings, job interviews and public speaking.

If you see someone who is slouching and round-shouldered, you might feel they are lazy or lacking energy.

Someone who is fidgety could come across as nervous, whereas folded arms can denote defensive behaviour. Of course human body language is complex and made up of an infinite variety of gestures, but it is worth being aware of how others see you. Although you may not be feeling lazy, nervous or defensive yourself, your default habits might give off signals of which you are unaware.

Have you ever studied yourself sitting and standing? Using a full-length mirror, check the position of your head, neck, shoulders, arms, back, hips, legs and feet.

What do you see? Look out for these common poor stances and positions: chin up in the air, collapsed neck, round shoulders, a dropped shoulder, displaced chest or hip, twisted pelvis, arched back, rounded upper back, asymmetry, sideways curvature of the spine, crossed legs, feet turned in or dropped arches. Why and how do we end up with such awkward postures? For some it's a lack of awareness, an accumulation of bad habits (such as having a kink in the back of the neck which seems to create an easy resting place for the head), or it's just gravity pulling us into lazy positions.

What posture should you see when you look in the mirror? You are aiming for three normal curves in the neck, upper and lower back areas, a well-balanced head and neck with ears over shoulders and top of the head towards the ceiling, a long back, tension-free square shoulders, arms hanging freely by your sides, hips facing straight forward, with your tummy tucked in and your bottom tucked under. Avoid pigeon toes, feet in ballet positions and fallen arches!

Much has been written about the benefits of good posture and how to achieve it, but one popular method practised by performers is the Alexander Technique. It is a system of body alignment developed in the 1890s by F. M. Alexander, an Australian actor who was plagued by vocal problems. Rather than change profession he decided to try and cure himself by observing in detail how he was using his body. He made changes to his posture that removed the tension and restrictions, so that ultimately he required less energy to project his voice.

The technique does not involve exercising, manipulation or hypnosis, but it works on the relationship between mind and body. In the same way that psychological anxiety is transferred to the body, so corrective thoughts can be used to retrain and eliminate old habits.

How does the Alexander Technique help presenters? The principle involves 'making spaces' in the body and the joints, as you 'grow taller and broader', which will create more space for the air you breathe in. Try sitting in a slumped fashion. It is much more difficult to breathe deeply when your upper body is crushed. Once you lift your body into an upright position you will be able to fill the lungs with air. Equally, if you are sitting or standing in a forced and rigid position, your breathing will be restricted by tense muscles.

A correct head position will help you to look the viewer directly in the eye, not down your nose or above the camera lens. A tiny tweak of the head position can make the difference between looking vaguely at the camera, and really looking at the centre of the lens. Not only that: with the average weight of the human head being around five kilograms, if you balance your head correctly the weight will be taken down the spine rather than on the neck!

I know many actors and singers who practise the Alexander Technique regularly to help keep their posture in check. You can go to a practitioner who will show you how to do it, and once you have learned the principles you can practise them at home. My first experience of Alexander Technique was memorable and quite extraordinary. The teacher gently placed my body in the correct alignment, and when she had finished both my earlobes started throbbing!

Some 'blockage' in my neck area must have been released and it seemed that blood had suddenly started to rush through!

Pilates offers another popular and safe set of exercises which restores balance to the body, and helps to achieve good posture. Born in 1880, eleven years after Alexander, Joseph Pilates was a frail, asthmatic child in Germany. He overcame his own condition by designing a series of mat and equipment exercises that elongated and strengthened the body. His system works on the core muscles which support the spine, and on correct breathing and precise muscle control. It was developed during the First World War as part of the rehabilitation process for injured veterans. Many devotees of Pilates claim that it has improved their body alignment and general fitness.

By looking in a mirror and studying your posture, habits of a lifetime may be revealed to you. What you are aiming for is to come across as open, relaxed and confident whether you use the Alexander Technique, practise Pilates, or just balance a book on your head!

## What can you do to relax?

Warm yourself up and chill out!

66 A few vocal exercises are always good, especially if you are going to be talking on air for a long period of time. Loosening the jaw and the body so you are relaxed and therefore more at ease on-screen with less tension can also help.

Louise Houghton, presenter, sit-up channels and *SuperCasino*

Much of the time we watch TV because we want to relax, to be entertained; but how can the viewer sit back and relax if the presenter is tense? The viewer wants to know that you, the presenter, are relaxed and in control – if you look stressed with a frozen face, stiff shoulders, a frown or a sweaty forehead, the viewer might be justified in reaching for the remote. So even if you are feeling a little tense, the trick is not to reveal it.

**❝** As long as I've been able to prepare beforehand, having warmed up, I'll try and find time to sit, relax and take a drink of water.

Howard Corlett, winner, *Sky Search for a Presenter*, 2006; presenter, *The Seven Wonders of the Weald* (Sky)

You should have a relaxed body to help create good performance technique in any discipline. Do you play an instrument, compete in sport, dance, act or sing? If so, would you consider performing a piece of music, playing a match, delivering a routine or a recital without first doing a warm-up? Although presenting is 'being you', it is still a bit of a 'performance'. Your body and voice will be going through a process similar to being onstage or performing. Just as a musician, athlete, dancer, actor or singer would do a warm-up for best results, so should you.

A relaxed, warmed-up body will not only be free from tension, it will facilitate deep breathing, because the muscles will be able to expand. So, here is that cycle of breathing deeply in order to relax, and relaxing to be able to breathe.

First of all, can you recognise tension in your body? Look in the mirror. Does your face look tense? Do you have a furrowed brow, a frown in your forehead, can you detect clenched teeth, raised shoulders, tense fingers? Or, do you see a relaxed, soft face, smooth forehead (age lines are acceptable!), loose jaw, shoulders down, and relaxed hands? Or maybe you are somewhere in between.

To relax the body you can try doing the following simple warm-up exercises. It's important to work particularly on the upper body – for breathing and voice production and because it is your upper body and face that are mostly in the frame.

☐ Stand up and stretch your arms above your head, reaching up as high as you can. See how tall you can make yourself by trying to touch the ceiling or the space above you. Use your arms alternately so that first one then the other tries to reach higher and higher. You are aiming to make your body as long as possible, and stretch out your back.

☐ Take your arms to the sides and stretch out sideways, trying to touch the walls or the spaces on either side of you. See how far you can reach out with your arms, hands and fingers. It's a good way of broadening the back and the shoulders. Shake out your arms and hands.

☐ Do some side bends from the waist, dropping down to either side with one hand by your side and the other reaching over your head in the direction of the bend. You are continuing to loosen up the body.

☐ You can also try twisting the body from side to side – keeping the hips facing front and twisting from the waist. Your hands can be kept on the hips, or let them swing round with the body. Again, this will help free up the body – with the added bonus of helping to keep the waistline trim!

☐ Rotate your arms one at a time in a large circle from the back of your body to the front. You are aiming to create a three-hundred-and-sixty-degree circle which will loosen up the shoulders. Try it again with the other arm rotating from the back to the front. Reverse the exercise and rotate your arms from the front to the back – again, one at a time.

☐ Try rotating your right arm forwards and simultaneously rotate the left arm backwards. It takes a bit of thinking about! Then try it the other way round, and rotate the left arm forwards while rotating the right arm backwards. Then give yourself a pat on the back!

☐ On to the shoulders. Shrug your shoulders up and down – try to touch your ears with your shoulders and then take the shoulders back down as far as they will go. When you are relaxed the shoulders should drop down into position, and be as far away from the ears as possible.

❑ Rotate the shoulders forwards then backwards in big movements. You may hear and feel crunching sounds, especially as you rotate the shoulders back – that is perfectly normal and is a sign that you have tension in the upper back. By doing these warm-up exercises you will gradually eliminate these tense knots in the muscles.

❑ To relax the neck, tilt the head forward and back, then incline your head from side to side, aiming for the ear to go as far towards the shoulder as possible. Then turn your head from side to side, trying to look over your shoulder whilst keeping your body facing the front. These movements will help to free up the neck area.

❑ A fun exercise to loosen up the neck is to draw an imaginary figure of eight in the air with your nose. Try doing it one way and then do it again in reverse – the bigger you make the movements, the greater the effect it will have.

The TV camera mostly concentrates on the face, so one good reason to have a face free from tension is to help you to have a natural smile and look confident on camera. Whether you are smiling or frowning, the camera picks up every expression on your face – usually in close-up!

❑ Make your face as tense as possible. Screw up your eyes, clench your jaw, make your mouth as small and tight as you can. Then do the opposite – yawn and smile broadly. What you're doing is manipulating the muscles and sensing the difference between a tense and relaxed state.

❑ Another good facial warm-up exercise is to imagine you are chewing an extremely sticky toffee. Use your tongue, cheeks and jaw as you pretend to chew the toffee. You can even open your mouth as you chew. Now imagine the sticky sweet is getting stuck in your teeth. Move your tongue around your mouth, as you try to get the imaginary sticky toffee off your teeth. Feel your whole mouth and jaw area loosening up – again the bigger you make the movements, the more beneficial the exercise.

❑ While waiting to go into an audition, many actors will rub their cheeks with their hands to free up the jaw area.

What you are aiming for is a relaxed, loose jaw, not a clenched jaw. I have seen presenters so tense around the mouth area that they look like ventriloquists!

If you are tense, especially in the upper body, neck and throat areas, you will constrict the larynx (the voice box) and could end up speaking with a voice in a higher register than you would ideally like. Whereas if that whole area of your body is relaxed and 'open', you will be able to start bringing down the register of your voice if necessary, and give yourself more authority. A high voice in a woman can sound 'little girly' and in a man can sound 'weak'.

As radio presenters and TV presenters rely on their voices for employment, and may be required to speak for hours at a time, they should warm up the voice and look after it too, so that it will sustain through the rehearsals and the recordings!

❑ Think about how sound is actually produced. The larynx houses the vocal cords which vibrate when air passes between them to make sounds or speech. One way of warming up your voice is to hum from a very low note to a very high note, and back down again; you should be able to feel the vibrations in your throat as you do this, and it will help to give your voice a varied pitch.

❑ Tongue-twisters are great fun and a really useful way of waking up the mouth and tongue. You will find tongue-twisters in voice books, and there are pages of tongue-twisters freely available on internet sites. Practising tongue twisters will also help you have clear diction.

You may have your own favourite warm-up exercises for body, face or mouth that are just as effective: mine are just suggestions.

At the beginning of your presenting career, or when going for auditions, I would suggest that you do plenty of physical preparation and warm up your body, face and voice. As you get used to presenting you may find you do not need as much preparation, but do not underestimate the amount of stress that can kick in when presenting in certain situations. You may feel fine at home before the shoot, you may know all your scripted lines perfectly and have sorted out the interview questions. However, when faced with a camera crew, real interviewees and a live transmission, you can lose the feeling of being in control of your nerves. That is why preparation is key, and you must develop techniques to quickly recognise nerves, recover your composure, think clearly and eliminate tension.

To have a relaxed face and upper body is not enough, you must be aware of tension throughout the body. I have seen presenters who look great in the close-up shot, but when the director cuts to a wide shot it reveals knee jerks and foot twitches that the presenter thought were out of shot!

How do other presenters relax?

66 Counting three, two, one, and feeling my body wind down. I also have an NLP (neuro-linguistic programming) anchor to help me relax.

Karin Ridgers, founder/presenter, veggievision.tv

## What is correct breathing?

Concentrate on how you're breathing while you are reading this. Where is the breath going to? Which part of your body is expanding and contracting? Have a look in the mirror and observe which areas of your body are moving when you breathe. If your upper chest and shoulder area is going up and down you could be breathing in a shallow way, and if the abdominal area below your ribcage is moving in and out you are breathing more deeply. Deep breathing is what you should be aiming for here.

What happens when you are nervous? Does your breathing change? Do you find your breathing becomes more of a chest movement, with emphasis on the upper part of the body rather than the lower? As already mentioned, one of the symptoms of stress is rapid and shallow breathing, as your body tries to cope with being in an uncomfortable situation.

Extreme nerves can lead to panic attacks or even hyperventilation, which usually means the person is taking lots of short breaths rather than breathing deeply using the diaphragm. It works both ways – by forcing yourself to breathe deeply you will counteract your nervous state and calm your body down.

Singers, actors, practitioners of yoga or relaxation techniques will all be familiar with deep breathing. Opera singers use their abdominal muscles to enable them to project their voices in large theatres and concert halls, and stage actors develop techniques to allow them to speak or sing whilst dancing or doing physical theatre. Disciples of yoga learn how to slow down their breathing rate to acquire a calm and meditative state. All this is achieved by knowing how to control your breathing.

❑ How do you breathe deeply and which muscles should you be using? To find the correct muscle group, place your hands under your ribcage with your fingers facing your belly button. Take in a deep breath and fill up with air – you are aiming to expand the area below your hands and you should be able to see it getting bigger. If you were lying flat on the floor with a telephone directory on your abdomen, it should be rising up and down as you breathe in and out. The shoulders and chest should not move and, in particular, when you breathe out the chest should not cave in. The body movement should be in and out rather than up and down.

❑ With your hands under your ribs, try breathing in slowly for five seconds, and slowly releasing the breath out through the mouth for five seconds. When you breathe in you should see and feel your hands moving apart as that area expands. When you breathe out, the area should contract and your hands should move closer together again. Once you have mastered this, do the exercise again, but try breathing in for eight seconds, and slowly release the breath through the mouth for eight seconds. You should find the process very relaxing and calming. The inhaled and exhaled breaths are related – if you have a short breath in, you will have a short breath out.

The muscles you need to engage are those that form the core stability in the tummy area. If you really expand these muscles as you breathe you should find you gain a feeling of being 'centred' and 'solid'. Not only will you feel more relaxed, you will develop the ability to build up a reservoir of air, which will sustain you through long periods of speaking aloud. On the other hand, if you breathe from your upper chest, you may not eliminate the nerves and you could run out of breath while presenting: your capacity to fill up with air will be less, and you may sound short of breath.

As you build up the strength in the diaphragm, you should find that delivering long speeches to camera will look effortless. Microphones are sensitive pieces of equipment and they can pick up every breath you take. It can become irritating for the viewer to hear noisy and frequent intakes of breath.

❑ To monitor your capacity for deep breathing, try singing a note aloud. Any note will do – it does not have to be a perfect Middle C. Just sing 'laaaaahhhhhhh' for as long as possible and see how many seconds you can sustain the note before running out of breath. How did you do? Did you go red in the face after ten seconds? If so, you could do with some more training. Did you make fifteen seconds? That's not bad. Repeat this exercise daily and monitor your progress. Aim to hold the note for at least twenty seconds. If you cannot do this, then keep practis-ing and you should improve – it's about working on a group of muscles and changing habits.

❑ Another exercise you could use to check your reserves of air is to read a long sentence aloud without pausing for breath – remember that this exercise is not about speaking with a good pace and pauses, it is a check to see how much you can read out loud without taking a new breath. Take a deep breath and read the following sentence:

'Well, that's just about all we've got time for today. I hope the weather's going to be fantastic wherever you are this weekend, and don't forget to try the chilli sauce on the barbecued burgers if you dare!'

How did you do? Did you get through it, or did you sound like you'd totally run out of breath? If you found it a challenge, try the deep breathing exercises regularly, and holding the note, then after a few days have another go at the above paragraph. If you managed to get through it without pausing for breath, add on the following sentence so that the exercise gets more challenging!

'Well, that's just about all we've got time for today. I hope the weather's going to be fantastic wherever you are this weekend, and don't forget to try the chilli sauce on the barbecued burgers if you dare! We're off to the sunny coast now to try and catch some mackerel. See you the same time next week, and until then it's goodbye from both of us. Goodbye.'

But remember – this is only an exercise in breath control. When it comes to presenting with a good pace and intonation, you will be expected to breathe and take pauses as necessary.

Deep breathing can be applied at any time and in any place, and others will not necessarily know that you are doing it. If you have any phobias such as spiders, getting in lifts or airplanes – or just stage fright – you will find that deep breathing will help you to get back in control.

Professional presenters use breathing techniques as part of their preparation – here are some of their thoughts on what techniques they employ:

66 Breathing exercises and visualisation... much like before a race!

Hannah McLean, commentator,
*FINA World Swimming Championships*, 2008

66 Shoulder rolls and deep breaths. Sometimes I go swimming if I have time.

Denise Ching, guest presenter, QVC

So, if you can develop the art of deep breathing it will help you to relax and to overcome nerves, and with good posture you should find it easier to look the camera square-on.

## What eyeline should you have?

How would you feel if the presenter you were watching stopped looking at the camera and started to gaze around the set whilst talking? The effect is that they have stopped looking at you, ceased to be interested in you or the subject, and the bond or connection between presenter and viewer is broken.

Your eyeline should be straight to the viewer, so most of the time a TV presenter should be looking directly at the camera – right into the centre of the lens. This is accepted 'TV grammar': if you analyse TV and study what presenters do, you will see that when the presenter is speaking to the viewer they will be looking to the camera most of the time.

Of course, there are exceptions to this rule. When a presenter is conducting an interview they will be looking at the interviewee, or when handling props it would be unnatural if the presenter did not look at the objects in their hands or on set. Some presenters will look down at their script for effect in between stories, just to break the eyeline for a moment and give a different feel to their presentation.

Another exception is co-presenting. Have a look at what presenters do when they are in this situation. On the whole they will be looking at camera even when they are not speaking. There are several examples of TV programmes that you can study to see how presenters do this; news programmes frequently have two presenters. In some ways it is harder to be the presenter who is not speaking. If you stare at the camera without any facial movement at all you may look frozen, on the other hand if you overreact you can upstage and be distracting. If you do nothing at all it can be interpreted as if you have disengaged from the viewer. When two presenters are sitting very close together it can look unnatural if one turns to look at the other because of their proximity.

What most presenters would suggest is that when you are not speaking you should look at the camera and mentally go through the script as if you were about to speak it, but do not vocalise it. 'Be in the moment' with your co-presenter and engage with the subject matter, but do not actually say anything.

Other genres of co-presented programmes such as daytime chat shows are good to study. The sets for these are usually more informal (often sofas), and the presenters may not be seated as close to each other. The rules are similar in that, if both presenters are in shot, the one not speaking will be generally looking to camera, but it is acceptable to look at the script for a few seconds, or at the co-presenter. I think you should be guided by the programme style and always think of how your actions will be interpreted by the viewer. Consider the context of the programme – what seems right in an entertainment show may well be completely wrong in current affairs.

You might be thinking that in real life we do not always look at the person we are speaking to all of the time, and you are right. Mostly people look at the person they are speaking to, but when they are thinking of the next thing to say they may look out of the window, at the floor or at the ceiling. When talking about a sensitive subject we may deliberately look 'into space', avoiding looking the other person in the eye. We can get away with this behaviour in real life because we are in the same room as the person we are speaking to and pick up other signals, such as body language, simultaneously. But when it comes to TV presenting, the viewer does expect the presenter to be looking at them almost all of the time, as this is how the presenter relates to the viewer. Whereas in real life you could carry on talking while looking at the table or the floor and get away with it, that does not work on TV. So, even when thinking of the next thing to say – keep your eyeline to the camera.

TV studios vary from the large and intimidating to not much bigger than a broom cupboard. Studio cameras can be big and cumbersome – some have a prompting device in front of the lens that enables the presenter to read the script whilst looking at the viewer. On the other hand, location camcorders are getting smaller and smaller. When you are presenting in close-up it will still be a close-up whether outside on the street in central London, a studio the size of a warehouse, or a small garage that is doubling up as a studio. It doesn't actually matter what size space you are presenting in or what size camera you are talking to, the rules about eyeline remain the same.

In real life, some people fix you in conversation and look directly into your eyes, almost staring without any variation in their gaze, and this can be unnerving. How can you talk to camera and look directly at the viewer most of the time without having a frozen stare or a 'rabbit caught in headlights' look? The answer is to be as natural as possible, blink if you need to, relax your face, and most importantly, smile.

## What is good diction?

**❝** Having trained as an actress and singer, I am no stranger to the wonders of the warm-up exercise! Tongue-twisters are great for getting your lips moving and ensuring you have crisp diction... now that's crisp diction, not a crisp addiction!

Nicci Brighten, presenter,
*Love Your Home Show*, 2008, Radio Wey 87.9 FM

Imagine you have finished the warm-up, prepared what you are going to say, but then, when you open your mouth, the vocal delivery is not as effective as it could be. Perhaps it sounds a bit dull, rushed, stilted, monotone, unconvincing or unclear. One of the skills and qualities a presenter must have is the ability to speak clearly, to convey information so that the viewer can understand it, to speak with enthusiasm and clarity.

The best way to assess your own voice is to listen to a recording of yourself, either on video or audio – bear in mind that it can be a bit of a shock! We are not used to listening to ourselves in this way, as when we speak we hear the sound resonate through our own head. I have worked with presenters with strong regional accents, nasal or constricted voices who do not realise how they actually sound until they hear themselves back. It does not matter if you have a regional accent, as long as it is not difficult for the rest of the population to decipher. To speak with received pronunciation, also known as RP (or 'the Queen's English'), is no longer a prerequisite for a presenter, but whatever your accent – whether you are like Welsh Huw Edwards reading *BBC News* or Ant and Dec from Newcastle presenting *Britain's Got Talent* – you must be intelligible.

To acquire good diction is something most people can do – it is a learned skill. Actors arrive at theatre schools with a whole array of native dialects, accents and speech defects, yet by the end of the course their voices will have changed in many ways. Their speech may be smoother, easier to listen to, more resonant with a lower register; actors can be trained to deliver lines in their native accent and other accents as required, but most importantly they will be able to speak very clearly.

Anyone can learn how to do this to some extent; you may not need to spend two or three years at drama school developing your voice. It certainly does help to have professional training, but there are lots of exercises you can do on your own, and any major bookshop will have dozens of books in their drama section on voice work. I have listed some good voice books in the Resources section in the Appendix.

Here are some basic exercises that will help you to get the most out of your voice.

❑ Open your mouth! If you do not open your mouth sufficiently when you speak, the words will not come out. It sounds fairly obvious, but it is amazing how many people have tense jaws and do not speak clearly because they are keeping the words to themselves. Presenters cannot mumble, they need to make sure the words are formed and that they are communicating them to the viewer. Although presenters use microphones, the microphone will only pick up the sounds that the presenters are making. So if you are making muffled, inarticulate noises, that is what will be recorded.

❑ Read passages from a magazine or newspaper aloud, and make a conscious effort to form each separate word and really use your lips and mouth to their fullest extent, going through all the vowel sounds. For example, when you make an 'oo' sound, push your lips forward as far as possible; when you make an 'aah' sound, open your mouth as wide as possible. These actions will loosen up the jaw area, remind you how to shape the words, and clarify diction.

❑ Yawning is a very good way of loosening up the jaw, and pretending to chew an enormous piece of gum is another useful exercise. Really work the jaw muscles so that they feel free from tension. We often have a clenched jaw without even realising it – in the same way that some people grind their teeth at night without knowing they are doing it – and this is a sign of tension. Try dropping the lower jaw away from the upper so that the lips are not tight together but have a small separation between them. This is the feeling of having a 'loose jaw', which you should practise so that you can recognise when the jaw has become locked into a tight position. I do not mean that you should walk around with your mouth open, but just become aware of when tension is creeping in and then counter it.

❑ If you are lazy with your speech, look for tongue-twisters which work on your weaknesses. To practise vocalising consonants in the middle or end of words, you should find tongue-twisters that feature those sounds such as 'getting' 'shopping' 'threatening' 'going' 'eating'. Without trying to lose your personality or background accent, you need to ensure the viewer receives the correct information. If you have poor diction, 'three' becomes 'free' and 'thought' becomes 'fought': mispronunciation can totally change the meaning of a script.

❑ The pencil exercise is great fun and really makes your mouth, tongue and jaw work hard. The principle is similar to the scene from the film *My Fair Lady*, where Audrey Hepburn's mouth is filled with marbles to help her change her accent from cockney to upper class. Instead of marbles you will need a pencil. First, find a tricky tongue-twister, then read it out loud. Try to pronounce every syllable, reading quickly but accurately.

For example:

'Royal lawyers, loyal lawyers, royal lawyers, loyal lawyers.'

Or:

'Three free flying thrushes, three free flying thrushes.'

Then put the pencil in your mouth like a horse's bit, so that it is horizontally behind your front teeth. Read the words again, forcing yourself to annunciate every syllable – without cheating! Take the pencil out of your mouth and read the words for the third time. Do you notice anything?

You should find that it is easier. This is not simply because it is the third time you've read the lines out loud. When the pencil is in your mouth it is causing an obstruction and forcing your jaw muscles and tongue to work much harder to pronounce every syllable. Once you remove the obstruction the muscles are able to move more freely – you have started to retrain them, to overcome lazy habits. So this proves you can train yourself to speak more clearly.

❑ What should you do if on hearing your voice back it sounds monotone or boring? One exercise actors do in theatre schools is to overemphasise words and fluctuation of the vocal register in order to retrain your speech habits. The theory is that if you 'overdo' it, you can then bring it back down to a natural tone once you have discovered how to overcome the problem.

Take any sentence or phrase, for example:

'I love going to the park.'

Try speaking it so that you elongate some of the vowel sounds, such as:

'IIIIII luuuuuuuve going to the paaaaaark.'

You should be aiming to overdo the sounds, and it will definitely not sound natural at this point. Aim to use the full range of your vocal register, from the lowest pitch to the highest. This kind of exercise will help you use the full potential of your voice and make it interesting to listen to.

❑ It is important to speak with passion – if you are enthusiastic about the topic then the audience will be too. One way to practise this is to speak about subjects you are really interested in. Start with ad libbing about topics such as your hobbies, holidays, pets or work, and experience what it is like to speak on a topic you can get excited about. When you are ready, record this exercise and play it back. Your voice and facial expressions should convey genuine enthusiasm. Remembering what this feels like, deliver a scripted piece to camera on another topic of your choice and check out how you now look when speaking. You should aim to carry the audience with you, even if the subject matter is not one of your personal favourites. Try to connect with the script, then you should be able to apply the same principles to all material that you are asked to present.

❑ You may not always be working with scripts and subjects that you feel passionate about. What happens if you are offered a presenting job on what you consider to be a dry topic, or an area you do not immediately connect with? When you are faced with a corporate script, how are you going to make it sound interesting? Think of it from the viewers' point of view – what is it that they need to know? What are the key points in the script that need to be portrayed? A script will have a purpose, a theme, that the producer or writer wants to get across. Find the main idea in each piece to camera that you've been given, and make sure you understand it; then go through the script and work out which are the key words in each sentence. Physically underline or highlight them, on your hard copy and/or on the prompt. As you come to those words you can give them a little emphasis to bring out the meaning of each sentence.

For example:

'Fairtrade shelves are made using wood from sustainable sources, from well-managed rainforests in Brazil. The farmers receive a higher percentage of the retail price, usually around twelve per cent, whereas in non-fairtrade deals the farmers can be left with as little as two or three per cent, which is not enough to live on. The issue remains that transporting this wood, even though it is fairtrade, is still contributing to climate change, as it is shipped from one side of the world to the other.'

The same script could be emphasised in the following way:

'<u>Fairtrade</u> shelves are made using wood from <u>sustainable</u> sources, from well-managed rainforests in Brazil. The farmers receive a <u>higher</u> percentage of the retail price, usually around <u>twelve</u> per cent, whereas in <u>non</u>-fairtrade deals the farmers can be left with as little as <u>two</u> or <u>three</u> per cent, which is not enough to live on. The <u>key issue</u> remains that transporting this wood, even though it is fairtrade, is <u>still</u> contributing to <u>climate change</u>, as it is shipped from one side of the world to the other.'

Another good exercise is to practise reading out reports from a newspaper – chosen at random!

❑ Bear in mind that when speaking on a topic that you find really interesting, you may start to speak too quickly. Also, nerves can make you speed up your delivery. Obviously it is important not to gabble or rush through a script or the audience will find it hard to follow what you are saying. Equally, it can be boring to listen to someone who is speaking too slowly. There is a rough guide within broadcasting of speaking at a rate of three words per second (there is more detail on this on page 64: 'How to talk to time').

To keep the viewer interested you will need to vary the pitch of your voice. As you make your way through the script, think of each paragraph and even each sentence as requiring a new thought and a new pitch. The way you modulate your voice has to be natural, and appropriate to the script or item. You can steal from the best – study the way the top newscasters read television news. As journalists they need to remain objective, not reveal emotions, and they cannot use their hands to gesticulate, so newsreaders use their voices to great effect, and can move from serious to light stories with ease. Study how they vary their pace and vocal range to convey change in mood.

Again, this could be rehearsed by choosing two contrasting newspaper reports to read out loud.

❑ If you are ad libbing, try to avoid 'ums' and 'ers'. We all litter our speech with these 'fillers' (they are hesitations we put in while we are thinking of the next thing to say), but when presenters overuse them it can weaken their performance, and take away from their authority as they sound unsure. Most people can learn how to eradicate 'ums' and 'ers'. To start with, try slowing down your rate of speech, to give yourself more thinking time. Or, try *thinking* the 'ums' and 'ers' without actually *vocalising* them. It will take about a second if you do this, and in that time you can smile at the viewer, then carry on talking, and no one will guess what you are up to. If you find your natural habits are hard to break, build up slowly. Start by talking for ten seconds without using 'ums' and 'ers', and when you can do that successfully, try speaking for twenty seconds, and so on.

Finally, it has been well documented that certain foods and drinks can help or hinder your voice production. Drink plenty of water, as speaking for long periods can give you a dry voice; TV studios can get very warm, and if you get dehydrated, your voice can sound cracked and you might 'lipsmack'. This is the sound of your tongue and lips making an audible, clicking noise as they part, usually at the beginning of a speech or in between sentences. Lipsmacks can be cut out in the editing suite, but not if the programme is live or your speech is littered with them! The main foods to avoid before using your voice are caffeine, milk and cheese, which can clog up the vocal cords.

**❝** I drink loads of tea, no milk, and cough... maybe a few 'lalala' notes and then... begin! No warm-up I'm afraid from me... tut tut!

> Jill Kenton, presenter, jnetradio.com, Hayes FM, QVC, *Dress My Mate*; contributor, *BBC Breakfast*

**❝** When talking to camera I try to concentrate on not talking too quickly so that I don't stumble over my words – which I can do when I talk too fast!

> Louise Houghton, presenter, sit-up channels and *SuperCasino*

Vocal training is a specialised area, and there are countless books on the topic – the Appendix has some suggested reading.

## What kind of energy do you need?

Do not assume that as a presenter you will be receiving lots of feedback and direction from the production team. You will be hired because you are right for the job, and you will be expected to just 'get on with it'. Any help you are given will probably be on script content and editorial ideas, rather than performance.

As production teams get smaller and more multiskilled, the director may have so many aspects of the production to look after he or she will have to assume the presenter can be trusted to get it right.

So how do you know when you are getting it right? What is the secret behind a successful presenting performance?

Many of the skills and qualities that a presenter requires have already been mentioned, but there is an elusive element to a performance, a certain 'wow' factor which is less easily defined. Some of the 'wow' can be described as energy. If you have the right energy for the TV screen, it will give your performance the edge and help your presenting to come alive.

Energy does not mean shouting or gesticulating with inappropriate movements. If you go the opposite way and try to counteract any 'theatrical' mannerisms, you can end up not doing enough. In an effort to be more real, you can find you have lost your energy and that your performance looks dull.

If presenting is about being you, why can't you just be yourself on camera? To some extent, that depends on how much energy you have in real life – but if you are yourself and nothing else, you could find your performance is lacklustre. You have learned to relax, but how do you prevent the performance from becoming too relaxed? You've been training to make your pieces to camera conversational – but is that enough?

The energy you require comes from being you, being relaxed and being conversational, but it is also a performance. You may need to hang on to some of that adrenaline pumping around your body to give yourself a 'ready to perform' feeling.

Remember your posture – sitting up straight or standing tall will give you energy. Your smile should help you to feel 'alive'.

Take every opportunity to record pieces to camera, watch them back and be objective. Even when you are a professional presenter you will still be improving as you gain experience, so ask for the recordings, review them and see if you can identify any residual weaknesses.

To give a performance more energy, speak with more enthusiasm. To make a performance more intimate try to imagine that the camera is a person in the same room as you. Ask yourself: would you want to watch your performance, or would you reach for the remote?

## What should you wear?

You will be judged by your appearance in the interview, screen test and performance. Think carefully about what statement you are making with your clothes, accessories and hair, what signals they give out and whether they are right for the programme and channel.

When you are invited for an interview or screen test, choose the look that is most appropriate for the production. If the audition is for a current programme, you can take your style ideas from the presenters on air, but if the programme is new, you can research the genre or channel. Some producers will include clothing guidelines in their pre-audition notes to you, but if not, don't be afraid to ask. When presenters are unsure about clothing I advise them to wear their best choice, but take with an alternative – if there is time before the actual screen test you could always ask the floor manager or a production assistant to give you their opinion. Channels and programmes will have a branding, a house style. Aim to walk into an audition looking just right for the production, so the producers do not need to second guess if you could fit in.

If there are specific instructions for clothing, the production team should communicate these to you beforehand. One obvious example is if chromakey is being used, also known as blue screen or green screen. This is where the presenter is placed in front of a blue or green screen and a different image is inserted, either live or in post-production, to add an idea of place, a company logo or stylised image. In chromakey techniques, wherever blue or green appear in the shot will be replaced with the new image, so you cannot wear anything of that colour. If you are presenting in a blue-screen studio, pretending to be in Paris, and the Eiffel Tower is to be added to the parts of the screen which are blue, wherever blue appears in shot will be replaced with the Eiffel Tower, even if that is your blue shirt!

Traditionally, certain fabrics and patterns are best avoided, as they do not work well on-screen. Although new cameras have different tolerances to older models, the guidelines are still worth bearing in mind. Stripes, dots, diagonals, herringbone patterns, can be too 'busy' on camera, too distracting, and sometimes interfere with the recorded image. Completely black or white clothes, especially around the neckline, can give the lighting director a hard time, as it can be tricky to expose against skin tones. It is best to steer clear of these designs and colours unless you check your outfit with the production team in advance.

Once you are employed as a presenter, consideration needs to be given to the set design and colour. The set designer may have used brightly coloured furniture such as lime green, in which case your clothing needs to be chosen with care to avoid clashes! Lighting designers, too, can use bright colours, but their gels can be changed more easily than the set-design colours. I have worked on a series where a costume designer took our presenter clothes shopping before the recordings took place, so that the correct look could be planned in advance, but this is usually restricted to celebrity presenters on high-profile programmes. Unlike television dramas, which do employ costume designers, most other kinds of television programmes will not have costume design in the budget, and presenters are required to select and use their own clothes. You cannot assume there will be an allowance in the budget for this.

It's always a good idea to check on costume requirements before a shoot – colours, styles, footwear – and have in your wardrobe a range of clothes for all presenting occasions that are likely to come your way. As with the screen test, you can bring a small selection to the rehearsal/shoot day, or at least an alternative option. Camera operators and lighting directors will look at the clothes on camera and let you know if they foresee a problem.

So, what should you have in your wardrobe? Certain colours are said to denote emotions – such as green for calmness and commitment, red for power. Your colouring could be described as autumn, spring, summer or winter; or you could try to assess your skin tone, your undertone, and relate it to your eye colour and natural hair colour – it can get confusing. There are companies, websites and consultants who will help you to dress for success, and advise on what colours suit you best. But don't let someone else's advice override your gut instinct. I was told that with my dark hair I could wear bright pink, so I bought a fluorescent pink fluffy dress, which I wore once and then it stayed firmly at the back of my wardrobe!

As well as tailoring your appearance to the production, dress in an appropriate way for your own colouring, body shape and age. Given that the head-and-shoulders shot is often used for presenting, the neckline is clearly in vision, so the colour and shape that is near to your face is important. Think about what suits your face shape best: V-lines or round-necked? Options for men are to wear a shirt buttoned up to the neck or unbuttoned; a tie; a formal jacket that helps to give a good line to the upper body; an unstructured jacket with a casual look; a T-shirt. Some presenters, such as John Craven and Frank Bough, are famous for wearing woolly jumpers! Make sure the viewer can see your face and eyes – don't hide under a long fringe or hair that flops forward. Most male presenters are clean-shaven, but if you have a beard or moustache, keep it tidy.

Avoid distracting jewellery and oversized earrings. As you turn from one camera or guest to another, large dangly earrings can swing around and become irritating. Necklaces that are too chunky may knock against a lapel mic, causing unwanted noise on the sound recording. Bracelets and bangles should be avoided as they can bang together, and if you are using a table they might clunk on the furniture. Some studios have certain rules about footwear, as stiletto heels can make small dents in the floor and prevent cameras from tracking smoothly across it.

The above points should also help you to decide what to wear on your showreel shoots. Treat the showreel shoot in the same way as a professional engagement, and you should look as if you have just been shooting the real thing.

## What if you are grey, wrinkly, mature or overweight?

Sometimes people ask me whether I think they are too old/fat/wrinkly/ugly to be a presenter, and my response is that if they have talent it will shine through. There are many examples of very successful presenters who could do with losing some weight, or who are mature, or not even that attractive. What matters is personality and confidence. If your physical appearance makes you feel uncomfortable, and you lack confidence because you are embarrassed about your looks, then you will not be at ease in front of the camera and the viewer will not feel comfortable either.

There have been some controversial discussions about ageism in the media, and in particular the lack of older women on TV screens. However, there are many characterful presenters on our screens in their sixties and beyond.

Within the area of children's programmes there were some notable 'grey-haired' presenters; for example, Johnny Morris and Tony Hart who presented BBC's *Animal Magic* and *Take Hart* respectively. Mature children's presenters can be seen as playing a maternal or paternal role.

If you are older than the average, but are an expert in a particular field, and have the necessary on-screen personality and presentation skills, you should be able to find employment. A quick search of talent agencies reveals many mature presenters who are sought after for their authority and knowledge. Bear in mind that other areas of media and broadcasting could also open up if you are an expert, such as after-dinner speaking and radio.

As previously mentioned, personal grooming is very important. Consider that a television presenter appearing on a screen in a viewer's house is a little like being invited into their home for a meal. In my view it does not matter if you are a touch overweight or greying round the temples, and you certainly do not need 'perfect' looks, but I would want to watch a presenter who is pleasing to the eye, and perhaps someone who one would actually like to invite round to dinner!

# PART THREE

# How?

## How to talk to camera

66 Talking to the camera is something that definitely gets easier the more you do it. People often say that it helps to imagine you are talking to one person down the lens. I don't have a particular person in mind, I just tend to view the camera as a friendly person.

Hermione Cockburn, science broadcaster, *Fossil Detectives*, *Coast*, *Rough Science*, *What the Ancients Did for Us* (BBC), Teachers TV

TV presenters talk to plastic and metal equipment on three legs or wheels – cameras. Although a TV actor is trained not to look at the camera, a TV presenter must look at the camera. The challenge is: how do you remain lively and animated when you are talking to an inanimate object? The presenter should seem like a friend, someone in the corner of your room, who's talking just to you.

66 I try to keep my TV-presenting performance natural by just remembering to be myself. I think at first I tried too hard to be what I thought was a 'TV presenter' – exaggerating everything, smiling all the time and shouting – where in reality it's just about treating the viewer as a single person and having a normal conversation with them. TV presenters shouldn't be 'actors', but just a gentle caricature of themselves.

Gemma Hunt, presenter, *Barney's Barrier Reef*, *Xchange* (CBBC); guest co-presenter, *Smile*

There may be six million other viewers all watching the same programme at the same time, but we tend to watch television as individuals or in small groups, so it should seem as though the presenter is talking to you individually. As the presenter, you should imagine the camera is a friend, and that you are talking to one or two people you know well, or typical viewers.

Smiles are very important.

66 I try to visualise an audience of one person behind the camera, I keep saying to myself 'smile', and I try to remember what's coming next.

Charlie Lemmer, presenter,
Real Estate Channel, Dubai Eye, Abu Dhabi TV, Current TV

You may be feeling perfectly happy inside, but not giving off enough signals for the camera to pick up. You need to smile – not a 'bolt-on' smile – but an inner radiance, a sunny personality which comes from enthusiasm and a connection with the script.

66 I think it helps that I'm not scared of the camera. I really enjoy what I do and try to imagine that I'm just talking to a few of my friends or members of my family. I also find a smile goes a long way to covering up any nervousness!

Becky Jago, presenter, *Anglia Tonight*, *Newsround*, *Sky Sports News*, GMTV's *Entertainment Today*

The same advice is given to radio presenters – talk as if you are chatting to one listener, and smile. The shape of your face changes when you smile and so will the sound of your voice. Try saying 'hello' with a frown, and 'hello' with a smile – it sounds different!

66 Smile before the camera cuts to you – it makes you appear warmer and friendlier than if the camera cuts to you and you have a straight face and then start talking.

Louise Houghton, presenter, sit-up channels and *SuperCasino*

What techniques do presenters employ when talking to camera to keep their performance natural?

66 As I am a very expressive person, I need to remember to 'tone down' my facial expressions.

Denise Ching, guest presenter, QVC

66 I've learnt to picture Kylie Minogue in my mind occasionally too, mainly to lighten my expression – but that's quite a nice thing to do anytime really.

Michael O'Donoghue, Higher Education producer/manager; presenter, Distance Learning TV

Bearing all that advice in mind, set up a video camera to record yourself in a head-and-shoulders framing. If you do not have access to a video camera, perform these exercises in front of a mirror. Remember the previous chapters – being you, eliminating nerves, posture, relaxation, breathing, eyeline, clear diction, energy, appearance, smile – and then start.

📽 Task 1

Tell the camera/viewer about yourself – speak for a couple of minutes about you, your hobbies or your current job.

How did you do? Play back the tape and analyse. Get used to watching yourself on video as a learning tool – and do not get sidetracked if you are having a 'bad hair day'. Imagine you are a viewer with a remote in your hand. Would you carry on watching this presenter, and if so, what is it that keeps you watching? Or, if you saw this presenter would you change channels, and if so, why? You could also ask a trusted friend or family member to 'mark' your performance with you – it could be very revealing. As you watch yourself back on tape, consider the 'Talking to Camera' self-assessment checklist (see page 196). You can photocopy it to use it again and again as you repeat the exercises.

📹 Task 2

Tell the camera/viewer a light-hearted story. Not a one-line joke and definitely not toilet humour! You are giving yourself permission to enjoy being in front of the camera and the effect should be that you speak with a twinkle in your eye and a natural smile!

Apart from newsreaders who should remain emotionally neutral, TV presenters in general should speak with a smile on their face – even weather presenters when telling us it is going to be unseasonably chilly with the possibility of snow!

View the recording back and analyse it with the checklist as before.

📹 Task 3

Tell the camera/viewer why you want to be a TV presenter, and if you are aiming for a particular genre, why? For example, why do you want to be a children's presenter or shopping-channel presenter? Use this as an opportunity to really think about what skills and qualities you can bring to the job, as if you were in a presenting audition or job interview. Play back the recording and criticise it using the checklist.

You should also start a video diary. You may have seen this concept on reality-TV programmes or documentaries. It is where the presenter or featured individual talks in an honest and candid style to the camera, revealing their day-to-day feelings or charting their progress on a particular challenge. You could set up the camera and talk to it on a regular basis, which will help to make the process more familiar: eventually it might become as easy as falling off a log!

These tasks should be repeated and played back until you feel really comfortable talking to the camera and your performance becomes easy and natural.

**❝** The key to keeping performance natural is down to practice. I am on air every day, which certainly helps to create confidence in front of the camera and allows me to be natural. I also record my shifts on air so I can watch myself back and see where I can improve.

Seema Pathan, presenter,
Price-drop TV, Bid TV, The Business Channel

**❝** I practise in front of a camera at home and watch myself. It is good to do this as you can spot any annoying habits – like saying 'okay' or 'now' too much. It takes a while not to be put off by the zero feedback from the camera lens.

Matthew Tosh, presenter, Teachers TV; guest presenter,
*Ministry of Mayhem* (ITV), *Brainiac Live: Test Tube Baby* (Sky)

To improve how you talk to camera, bear in mind the following points:

- Before you present, repeat the exercises in relaxation, posture, breathing, diction and pace to train your body, voice and mental skills.
- Do the exercises in talking to camera, recording to video and analysing the playback several times.
- Look at your performance critically.
- You should see improvements as you get used to the process, but it won't be perfect straight away.
- Keep watching professional presenters and really study what they do – learn from the best.
- Show your recordings to friends and family and tell them to be absolutely honest in their opinion.
- Make a video diary every day, look back at the older recordings and see how you have developed.
- At this stage you might be feeling, 'I cannot do this' or 'I can nearly do this.' So keep practising until you feel really confident talking to the camera.

**❝** You, the presenter, are delivering information that the viewer wants to learn, so make it exciting and fresh. Remember to smile and enjoy your work as the viewer can feel and see this. There is nothing worse than seeing a bored television presenter. Be engaging and make sure the viewer doesn't want to turn to another channel!

Jill Kenton, presenter, jnetradio.com, Hayes FM, QVC, *Dress My Mate*; contributor, *BBC Breakfast*

## How to talk to time

As a presenter, you will need to 'talk to time', in other words, to be able to speak for a specific duration, whether ten seconds or ten minutes. Why? Most television and radio programmes are designed to fit a particular gap in the schedules, whether it's a five-minute or sixty-minute slot. You might think a five-minute programme would fill a five-minute slot, and a sixty-minute programme would fill an hour – but you would be wrong!

A thirty-minute slot on BBC1 may contain a programme of twenty-eight minutes and twenty-five seconds, plus trailers for other programmes and channel idents, which make up the remaining duration to fit the slot. A half-hour programme on ITV may only be twenty-four minutes and thirty seconds, to allow time for trailers, channel idents and, of course, commercials before, during and after the programme. It is the responsibility of the production team – the producer, director or production assistant – to deliver a programme of the correct duration, as agreed with the channel, so that the channel can adhere to the advertised schedule as far as possible.

If you are presenting a live programme you will be given timings to guide you through to the end of the programme, and you will be expected to stop talking elegantly just before 'zero' – without the viewer realising you've been asked to 'wind up'. Even if you are working on a pre-recorded programme, there may be good reasons why you will be asked to talk to time; the programme might be recorded 'as live' for a transmission later that day, or editing time might be limited.

Here is a sample running order for a live gardening programme, *Cottage Gardening – Live*. It is just under fifteen minutes in duration and will fit into a fifteen-minute slot in the schedules.

| STORY NO | ITEM | FORMAT | DURATION |
|---|---|---|---|
| 1 | Titles | VTR | 00.00.17 |
| 2 | Main intro | Pres IV + overlays | 00.00.32 |
| 3 | Awards | MH VTR | 00.03.00 |
| 4 | Sting | VTR | 00.00.05 |
| 5 | Interview 1 (CC) | Pres IV + 1 | 00.02.00 |
| 6 | Sting | VTR | 00.00.05 |
| 7 | Hollyhocks intro | Pres + 1 | 00.00.15 |
| 8 | Hollyhocks | MP VTR | 00.02.00 |
| 9 | Sting | VTR | 00.00.05 |
| 10 | Allotments Intro | Pres IV | 00.00.15 |
| 11 | Allotments | VTR | 00.02.00 |
| 12 | Sting | VTR | 00.00.05 |
| 13 | Vox pops intro | Pres IV | 00.00.15 |
| 14 | Vox pops | VTR (HD) | 00.01.00 |
| 15 | Sting | VTR | 00.00.05 |
| 16 | Interview 2 (F&S) | VTR | 00.02.00 |
| 17 | Sting | VTR | 00.00.05 |
| 18 | Goodbye | Pres IV + Grfx | 00.00.25 |
| | | TOTAL | 00.14.29 |

What does the above running order mean? There are some standard abbreviations used in TV running orders and scripts:

VTR    Video-tape recording.

IV    In vision.

OVERLAYS    Pictures floated over the top of the presenter's voice, so the presenter becomes 'out of vision' for that section.

STING    Musical bridge with animated pictures to separate parts of the programme.

GRFX    Graphics.

VOX POPS    From the Latin 'vox populi' which translates as 'voice of the people'. Vox pops are unrehearsed, quick interviews with the general public to get the point of view of the 'man on the street'.

This particular script has some abbreviations which would be specific to this production:

MH    Melanie Harris, whose award-winning garden is featured in a video item.

HOLLYHOCKS    The name of the video item shot in MP's (Mary Powell's) garden.

ALLOTMENTS    The title of a video item.

Other capital letters are initials of presenters and contributors.

The commissioning editor or executive producer will have told the producer how much money is in the budget, how many programmes are needed, and of what duration, to fill the programme schedules. The producer may start with a blank piece of paper and has to create programmes to fit the brief. If the slot is fifteen minutes, then the completed programme cannot exceed that duration. That is why *Cottage Gardening – Live* is calculated to run at fourteen minutes twenty-nine seconds, although sometimes the channel will agree a short overrun or underrun.

Here is another sample running order from *Why I Did It* –
an in-depth interview programme, where the interviewee
reveals why he or she took a controversial course of action:

| STORY NO | ITEM | FORMAT | IN | OUT | EST DUR | ACTUAL | CUM | ACTUAL |
|---|---|---|---|---|---|---|---|---|
| 1 | Pre Title | Pres IV | | | 00.00.08 | | 00.00.08 | |
| 2 | Titles | VTR | 10.00.00 | 10.00.13 | 00.00.13 | | 00.00.21 | |
| 3 | Main Intro | Pres IV + Aston | | | 00.00.37 | | 00.00.58 | |
| 4 | Package | VTR + Aston | 10.01.00 | 10.04.48 | 00.04.48 | | 00.05.46 | |
| 5 | Discussion | Pres + 1 | | | 00.21.44 | | 00.27.30 | |
| 6 | Goodbye | Pres IV + Grams + Aston | | | 00.00.30 | | 00.28.00 | |
| | TOTAL | | | | 00.28.00 | | | |

ASTON    The machine that puts names on the screen.

GRAMS    Sound effects, such as closing music.

EST DUR    Estimated programme duration.

CUM    Cumulative duration.

ACTUAL    Actual programme duration.

This programme consists of the pre-title tease, titles, introduction to the topic, video item to explain the background
to the story, and the main thrust of the programme is the
presenter + 1 discussion (Story 5), which is the presenter
and the interviewee. The interview itself runs for just under
twenty-two minutes, and the total running time for this
half-hour slot is a twenty-eight-minute programme.

So speaking to time is crucial, but how do you learn this
skill?

❏ Start by breaking timings down into small units.

   On the basis that broadcasting speech should be approximately three words per second, a ten-second piece to

camera will be about thirty words. Here is a simple, thirty-word script:

'Well, that's just about all we've got time for. Hope the weather's going to be fantastic wherever you are this weekend, and until next time it's goodbye from us. Goodbye.'

Try reading the above script aloud and time yourself. If it takes you nine or ten seconds that is spot on! If you took a lot less than ten seconds – around seven or eight seconds – you are speaking too quickly. On the other hand, if you took longer than ten seconds – say twelve – you are speaking too slowly.

The above rule is a useful one to check your speaking rate, to see if you are really speeding through scripts or speaking at a snail's pace. However, it is only a guide. A ten-second script using long words with many syllables will need fewer words to fill the time, and a script using lots of very short words may need more words.

In television, the timing of the script is more important than the word count. So if you are asked to write a ten-second script, write thirty words and time it. Then it's a judgement call – if you feel you are speaking at an acceptable rate and the timing comes in at less than ten seconds, you could try speaking more slowly, or add some more words. If your script reads at over ten seconds, try speaking more quickly or delete some words. Remember, the 'three words per second' rule is only a guideline.

❑ Try reading this next example out loud and see the difference for yourself – it is still thirty words, but the timing will alter depending on the types of words you use.

'Unfortunately, that's all we've got time for in today's programme. The weekend is predicted to be fantastic weather, so maybe you could try barbecued sweetcorn! Goodbye from Henrietta and me.'

The above example uses several multisyllable words and takes about twelve seconds to read aloud.

What should you do if, during rehearsal, the script takes ten seconds to read, but on the recording or live transmission you become nervous and speak too quickly, finishing the script too early? If you have about one second to fill, then smile! Or, knowing that three words make one second, you could add a phrase to fill the time. Here are some commonly used ones:

- 'Bye for now.'
- 'See you later.'
- 'After the break…'
- 'Join us then.'
- 'Don't go anywhere.'
- 'Join me tomorrow.'

If you watch television closely, or listen to the radio, you will become aware of how presenters manipulate time in this way. BBC Radio 4 is a good example of how presenters talk to time. It is a speech-based radio channel and it plays the 'pips', a pre-recorded sound effect to mark the start of each new hour. If there is a live programme or link before the pips, you will hear how the presenters either speak slower or faster to finish on time. The aim is not to 'crash' into the pips.

Have the confidence to slow down or speed up as necessary, to ad lib and throw in extra phrases if you need to, rather than staring at the camera, praying for the seconds to tick away if you have finished your script early.

You may leave out a section of the script altogether by mistake and finish with several seconds to spare – a three-word phrase will not be enough to fill the time. Bear in mind that although some of the production team know what the script should be, the viewer does not. If you have left out a chunk of script, fill the time you have with relevant material. Hopefully you will be familiar with the aim of the script, and will be able to ad lib, fill the required slot on the running order and make sense.

☐ Practise ad libbing to time on a variety of topics. Watch the clock and see if you can happily chat, without running out of things to say. Gradually increase from one minute, to two, then three minutes. I know presenters who practise ad libbing about a ketchup bottle for two minutes – the possibilities are endless! Do remember to make sense. You can check the later sections on interviewing, children's makes and shopping channels to learn how to structure what you say.

☐ You could write short, timed scripts, memorise them and deliver them to camera, checking that they fill the time slot. Start with ten-second scripts, then twenty-second scripts (which would be about sixty words). Continue to extend and challenge yourself until you can comfortably write and memorise thirty seconds, forty seconds and even one minute. There are some timed script examples in the Appendix for you to practise with. It is not uncommon for a presenter to speak to camera from memory for one minute – have a look at television programmes made on location, which probably do not use a prompt, and see for yourself.

## How to memorise scripts

66 Working as an actor as well, I have to learn scripts at short notice all the time – the more you do, the better you get at it. I think of the journey of the story as I go through, which helps me to help learn scripts.

Howard Corlett, winner, *Sky Search for a Presenter*, 2006; presenter, *The Seven Wonders of the Weald* (Sky)

Just as TV scripts can be written very quickly, you may be asked to learn them equally fast – so it does help to have a good memory. Unlike theatre productions, where a script is rehearsed over several weeks, a TV script will need to be memorised in hours or even minutes. So how do other presenters approach this task?

**❝** For me, the best way to memorise a script is through repetition and saying the words out loud. It's not enough to read them through in your head, you need to vocalise the words and hear how they sound spoken aloud. After all, that is the essence of presenting. Associating the words with images or emotions also helps. Another good way is to use cue words to help trigger your recall.

Nicci Brighten, presenter,
*Love Your Home Show*, 2008, Radio Wey 87.9 FM

On a regular weekly magazine programme the research will be done up to the last minute and the studio script might not be finalised until the day before recording. It is quite possible that the presenter may not receive the scripts until then. Sometimes the scripts are handed to the presenter in make-up!

**❝** I break the script into sections and learn each part. Once I have learnt one part I move on to the next. If I can get the script the day before I always do to give me more time to learn it.

Seema Pathan, presenter,
Price-drop TV, Bid TV, The Business Channel

If a prompting device is used there will be no need to actually memorise the scripts. Unfortunately, not all TV studio recordings use a prompt – there may not be enough money in the budget, and some presenters and producers prefer a more informal approach. You will rarely find a prompting device on location. They can be cumbersome to move from one set-up to another, and in these days of diminishing crew numbers, it can be time-consuming to pack, rig and de-rig the prompting equipment. On location you might be presenting as you walk from a distant point towards the camera, so you would have to rely on your memory – even if there was a prompt you wouldn't be able to read it until you were close enough! It is reasonable to assume that during your career as a presenter you will be asked to learn scripted material, possibly under pressure.

**❝** I learn the words quickly! Almost by just taking a mental snapshot of the words and noting the actual points and their logical sequence, which makes it easier to remember.

Renée Castle, presenter, Caribbean New Media Group,
Caribbean Communications Network,
Sun Community Television

Equally, you must grasp the point of the script.

**❝** I make sure I understand the content of the script first so that if I stumble I'm able to improvise a little. I read a section, memorise it and read it back to myself aloud. The more comfortable you are with the text, the easier it is to present it.

Naomi Evans, presenter,
Ravensbourne College in-house training courses

Unfortunately, learning the script doesn't always pay off. Imagine you have been asked to shoot a piece to camera about shopping habits in a busy shopping street. You have been given a script by the producer the night before the shoot, which you've learned thoroughly, but when you arrive at the location the researcher receives a call from the executive producer wanting changes. Your piece to camera is hastily rewritten and you have to relearn it. What will you say? 'I can't learn this new script in a hurry,' or 'I spent ages learning the old script,' or 'My mind is so full of the previous version I am getting confused' or 'No problem, give me five minutes and I'll sort it out'?

You need to practise learning material quickly because that is the professional approach. Here are some more techniques that other presenters use:

**❝** I memorise the sound of a passage as much as the content, so I read it aloud a number of times. Also pick out key words which link one sentence to the next, and use them as 'hooks' to lead you into the next line.

Helen Percival, presenter,
Ravensbourne College in-house training courses

**❝** I like to rewrite where possible, so it's in my own words. That makes it easier.

> Cate Conway, presenter, *The Seven Thirty Show* (UTV),
> *Cooking in the Community* (Northern Visions)

**❝** I practise! I usually have a scan of the scripts when I first get them, at least a day ahead of the shoot. I would then read through chunks of the script several times, to become really familiar with it. Then the most important thing for me is to put it down and go and do something completely different, like have dinner. I'd then come back and read the chunk again. Each time I take a break, I leave it longer and longer – this forces your brain to dump it into the long-term memory. If the scripts are given to me just before a shoot and I know which bit we are doing first, then I would read it several times and start to repeat each sentence quietly to myself. It is okay to stand off-set, muttering lines to yourself. I've seen other presenters do it and people would rather you did this than not know your lines at all! At the end of the day, everyone will develop their own strategies for learning scripts.

> Matthew Tosh, presenter, Teachers TV; guest presenter,
> *Ministry of Mayhem* (ITV), *Brainiac Live: Test Tube Baby* (Sky)

Is it important to remember the script verbatim (exactly word for word), or is it acceptable to paraphrase and just deliver the sense of the script? You should check with the producer you are working with, but as a general rule it is fine to rearrange words as long as the script still makes sense. The main exception to this is hard, factual items where the information must be accurate, and corporate scripts where the copy might have been checked by lawyers or those responsible for language style.

One of the above presenters refers to 'rewriting the script'. It can be easier to learn your own words rather than those written by someone else – again, first check with the producer. Techniques that work involve highlighting key words and making links in your mind from one section of the script to the next. Another is to write out the script in longhand, and then keep reading it out loud to practise it over and over again.

Speaking from experience, I would advise that you keep the script with you during the rehearsal and recording process. Literally sit on it, so that you can whip it out and continue to learn it while camera, lights and sound are preparing and checking; then when the director is ready for a take, pop the script out of sight, or sit on it again! An unpopular presenter is one who leaves the script in their dressing room or bag, then needs to unclip the radio mic and leave the set to retrieve it, wasting valuable time.

Make sure you understand the script, otherwise it is very difficult to learn, recall and communicate it to the viewer. If you understand it, even if you forget some of the words or phrases, you will still be able to ad lib on the topic and get the message across, and, more importantly, get to the end of the script.

Like an actor learning lines, you will need to know the script one hundred per cent, as this will help you to cope with any distractions on set. The more familiar you are with the script, the less likely it is that the viewer will realise you are speaking from memory.

## How to write scripts

66 I would write a script or piece to camera in a way people can relate to from the armchair. It's easy to change the channel, so keep them watching by engaging them in the conversation – don't make it easy for them to turn the channel over. Make it exciting and fun.

Jill Kenton, presenter, jnetradio.com, Hayes FM, QVC, *Dress My Mate*; contributor, *BBC Breakfast*

TV scripts can be written in a variety of styles, ranging from narrative documentary to chatty entertainment, but on the whole TV scripting is more conversational than print would be. Printed material, such as newspapers or magazines, can have more complex sentences than TV scripts because they are read 'in your head'. Once you start to speak the sentences aloud it becomes clear that a more informal style is required for broadcast.

One simple check for this is to write yourself a script and read it out loud. Have you written any phrases that are tricky to speak? Any hidden tongue-twisters? Or, if someone else has written the script for you (for example, a member of the production team), they may not have read the script aloud to themselves, and could have unwittingly written something that is hard to speak. Check every script you're given in this way. I have come across people who can write brilliant scripts – witty, full of attitude and style. However, when they try to deliver them to camera they can come unstuck, because they fell into the trap of not practising aloud.

If the script is to be read from a prompting system, avoid long sentences which are hard to read as the whole sentence may not be visible on the monitor. There are always exceptions to the rule and you may find that some presenters read complex scripts fluently – either written by themselves or others – but they are probably very experienced at their craft!

Where do script ideas come from? Some presenters are given scripts written by the production team; some presenters are part of the production team themselves, sourcing ideas, researching and writing their own scripts; good ideas can also come from the producer, commissioning editor, director or even the runner. You should write some sample scripts, perhaps for a showreel, from ideas driven by your own interests.

Whatever the style, a good script will engage the viewer, be informative, interesting, and consider the basic elements of who, what, why, where and when. Think about what information will be given in the studio introduction, what will be in the item itself or delivered from the location, and how the elements link together.

TV producers, directors and researchers are used to writing scripts very quickly, and they may expect you to write scripts quickly too. A simple way to practise is to take a topic you are familiar with, such as weather, sport or shopping, copy the format and style used on everyday programmes, but rewrite it in your own words. If you are asked to write a piece to camera, do your research into the topic and try to find an interesting peg or angle.

A TV script goes through several stages, with the director adding camera instructions at a certain point. The final format could look something like this example below, or it could be in two columns with the dialogue on the right-hand side of the page and the camera instructions on the left.

---

HAMPSTEAD GARDEN SUBURB

PRESENTER STANDS OUTSIDE NO. 1 SOUTH SQUARE & READS PLAQUE ON THE WALL. CU PLAQUE THEN CAMERA FINDS PRESENTER

PRESENTER (READS PLAQUE)

Dame Henrietta Barnett lived here from 1915 to 1936. Founder of Hampstead Garden Suburb.

PRESENTER TURNS TO CAMERA

And what a perfect place to live – right in the centre of the suburb which she founded over one hundred years ago.

PRESENTER WALKS TO CAMERA

I'm only seven miles from the centre of London and it feels like I'm in the countryside. That was part of Dame Henrietta Barnett's vision – when she described the design of the suburb she said:

'Great care will be taken that the houses shall not spoil each other's outlook. The houses will not be put in uniform lines or without consideration for picturesque appearance.' She definitely succeeded.

---

---

PRESENTER EXITS FRAME

CENTRAL SQUARE

PRESENTER ENTERS FRAME

Hampstead Garden Suburb is internationally recognised as one of the finest examples of early twentieth-century domestic architecture and town planning.

It was Henrietta's dream to build a community where rich and poor could live side by side. She had witnessed the extreme poverty in London's East End, and vowed to create a tranquil and leafy environment for all.

The suburb has two churches, designed by Sir Edwin Lutyens, a Quakers' meeting house, a synagogue, two woods, tennis courts and, behind me here, the Institute for Adult Education – now the famous Henrietta Barnett School.

PRESENTER EXITS FRAME

ERSKINE HILL

PRESENTER WALKS TO CAMERA

Part of the suburb's charm is that there are no fences – only hedges are allowed. And when each house was built, fruit trees were planted in every garden.

The suburb today is maintained with great care by the Trust, so it looks almost exactly as it did when it was built in 1907.

PRESENTER EXITS – PICTURE FADES TO SEPIA

---

66 The first thing to do is the background research. This is sometimes done by a researcher, who will give me some starting points. At other times, I have to do this myself. I always write in the style that I speak. Often I'll have an idea of what I want to say, and so I'll say it out loud, as if talking to someone. This gets put down on paper. Then I'll read through it in real time, checking it against a stopwatch to see if I am likely to run under or over. The challenge is knowing how much to put in or leave out! For this, I need to imagine that I know nothing about the subject – could I get a good gist from reading the script?

Matthew Tosh, presenter, Teachers TV; guest presenter, *Ministry of Mayhem* (ITV), *Brainiac Live: Test Tube Baby* (Sky)

**66** I firstly have to know how long my script needs to be so I can work within a time frame. I also think the key to a good script is not to overcomplicate it – keep it simple.

Seema Pathan, presenter,
Price-drop TV, Bid TV, The Business Channel

## How to present in studios and on location

The environment in which you are presenting can play a part in your ability to deliver scripts to camera. In your career you will need to be able to present in TV studios and locations.

**66** Are you headstrong, independent and like to be out and about? Perhaps you like a more controlled atmosphere in the cosy comfort of indoors. Maybe you're a mixture of both. As a presenter you need to literally be prepared for anything – rain or shine. There is a certain safety about being in the studio – outside it's a big, bad world, but it's also an exciting one. For me, it's all about location, location, location.

Nicci Brighten, presenter,
*Love Your Home Show*, 2008, Radio Wey 87.9 FM

As a presenter you may find yourself presenting in a warm studio, with a big production team to look after you; in a windy exposed field, with no creature comforts; in a bustling capital city; or on a remote island beach. The decision to shoot in a studio or on location, at home or abroad, will be taken by the production team, and depends on a number of factors such as the production budget, the delivery date, and the demands of the script. Here are some of the differences – and similarities – between presenting in a studio or on location, so you can prepare for either eventuality.

Studios are usually soundproofed, air-conditioned, well-maintained, purpose-built, high-tech recording spaces. There might be a large production team including several camera operators, floor managers, production assistants, director, producer, executive producer, costume department, make-up artists, vision mixer, engineers, cable bashers, prompting devices and operators, graphic designers, set-design team, sound recordists, lighting director, riggers and runners.

Traditionally, studios are highly controlled spaces, with no natural daylight, no outside noise, heavy doors, and a lighting rig. But a studio could be a converted church with no frills, broken air-conditioning, and a small team of multi-skilled personnel, where you will be asked to do your own make-up. It's all down to budget. In general, however, a studio will have more equipment and a larger team of people than you will find on location.

Television studios usually have multi-camera set-ups, so you may have more than one camera framed up on you at once. For a 'chat show on the sofa' format, it is not uncommon to have four or five cameras being used at the same time. Usually these cameras are manned by an operator, but increasingly some channels are using remote cameras operated by technical staff in the control room, so it is possible that you could be speaking to a camera that does not even have anyone standing behind it. In some shopping channels and interactive gaming channels, all the cameras might be remotely operated, so you could be in the studio all by yourself. There may not be a floor manager, and it is possible that you might be asked to operate the prompt yourself; on some late-night shifts in regional newsrooms you could be the only person in the studio. So studios can range from very busy places to rather lonely ones. Even if the camera is not manned, you still need to talk to the viewer via the lens – do not become a robot yourself!

In a multi-camera set-up, the shots are edited in real time through the vision-mixing desk, either by the director or a separate person, the vision mixer. The director will preview all available shots such as a close-up of the presenter, a two shot of the presenter and interviewee, and a wide shot of the studio. You will know which camera to look at as the segment will have been rehearsed or talked through beforehand; additionally the information can be written on the prompt and you can receive instructions through your earpiece. The selected camera will display a red cue light, or tally light, so if you are talking to a camera with a red cue light that is not on, you are talking to the wrong camera!

From a presenter's point of view, as long as you are talking to the right camera, it should not make any difference to your performance which camera you are speaking to. You should do a natural head turn to each camera as instructed, and carry on talking – whether it is a close-up camera, the two shot or the wide shot. As you turn your head, the vision mixer will cut from one camera to the next, and the red light on the selected camera should be visible to reassure you that you are speaking to the correct camera.

**❝** I like the variety and buzz of having more than one camera in a studio. There's no other environment quite like it. It is more pressured as you feel that if you make a mistake, you will be letting more people down. On single-camera shoots, I find that I can build up a much closer working relationship with the camera operator. It is always important to establish a good relationship here! I quite like being out on location too – every location is different and it's fun to see how the passers-by react to you filming. I once did a long shot in amongst a crowd of people, with the camera on a balcony about thirty metres away. Of course, as soon as I got the signal, I had to start talking to camera, and with conviction. Not many people could see where the camera was and a number of people around me thought I was talking to them. It made me chuckle afterwards.

Matthew Tosh, presenter, Teachers TV; guest presenter, *Ministry of Mayhem* (ITV), *Brainiac Live: Test Tube Baby* (Sky)

Unlike multi-camera studios, when you are on a location shoot, such as a documentary, you will usually find just one camera, and probably without a prompting device.

66 I love working with a single camera on location... there is something about the outdoors and a camera that makes you smile more. Studio work can feel a little staged and scripted!

Jill Kenton, presenter, jnetradio.com, Hayes FM, QVC, *Dress My Mate*; contributor, *BBC Breakfast*

Single-camera shooting means one shot is recorded at a time, and edited together later. The close-up shot of the presenter introducing the topic could be one set-up, then the camera operator could reposition the camera to frame up for the interview, and the wide shot might be done from yet another position. All the recorded material will then be taken to the editor who will cut it together to make a seamless sequence.

What this means for a presenter is that you may have to hold information in your head for long periods of time as the crew reposition the camera, check the framing and sound levels for each new set-up. Rather than delivering a long piece to camera from one position, you may need to start it in one place and finish it in another. On the other hand, this way of working can give you the opportunity to check you are comfortable with every section of script before you record.

66 Location shoots can be hard work as you are often walking around a lot, although they can be more spontaneous than studios as the crew find the good locations to record the links. There are other elements that come into play, like noise and sunlight affecting the shots. It's important to know what you are doing and saying as a presenter as, no doubt, you will have to do take after take because of factors outside your control.

Louise Houghton, presenter, sit-up channels and *SuperCasino*

Whether in the studio or on location, the script may not be shot in order, and it is very common for location shoots to be shot out of sequence. Availability of a particular location, or interviewee, the position of the sun, the tide timetable, proximity to a good lunch venue, parking – any factor could dictate what is the most practical shooting order for the day or even the series. You may find the opening piece to camera is recorded at the end of the day, or at the end of several weeks' shooting, and that the final piece is shot before anything else. This is a similar situation to that of an actor taking part in a film – shooting out of sequence is the norm in film-making where complex schedules rely on the availability of actors and locations.

How does this affect the presenter? You need to be aware of your continuity so that shots recorded over several different days or weeks can still be cut together seamlessly in the edit. Physical continuity is, for example, remembering which hand you used to hold your hat as you walked over the hill, and emotional continuity includes your feelings when you, for example, saw the tomb for the first time.

It is worth mentioning continuity so that you are aware of it when rehearsing and recording – especially in single-camera set-ups. When shots or scenes are edited together, the action must appear continuous and logical. Slam the door with the wrong hand and your best performance may never get used because the editor couldn't make it fit with the previous shot. Exit too soon and your most energetic take could land up on the cutting-room floor. Did you take a sip of coffee before or after you said 'Hello and welcome'? Good continuity makes you popular and appear professional. Poor continuity wastes good performances and precious shooting time.

Continuity is important even in studios and multi-camera shoots. During camera rehearsal the camera operators, lighting director, sound supervisor, director and vision-mixer check shots, camera positions and props. Once this is sorted they assume it will stay exactly the same for the take, and if you make a change between the rehearsal and the recording without telling anyone, the recording may go wrong.

Some large-scale shoots that take place outside of the studio are known as outside broadcasts (OBs), typically a discussion programme, an event, sports fixture, concert or festival. Long-running OB series include programmes as diverse as BBC's *Question Time* and *The Antiques Roadshow*. They are multi-camera and set up like a studio, with control rooms in trucks known as scanners, but the location is not an actual studio – it could be a church or town hall. When you are working on an OB it is like being in a studio, but on location.

Wherever you are presenting you should remember that the size of the lens and the scale of the environment should not affect your relationship with the camera and the viewer. On the whole, most shot sizes of presenters are mid-shots, (head and shoulders), and the microphone will be either on your lapel or on the desk, so as a presenter you do not need to try any harder just because the surroundings are 'big'.

There are many potential distractions in a studio. Imagine you are presenting an unrehearsed, rolling magazine or current-affairs programme, or a shopping channel, live on air for hours at a time. Studio guests will be coming and going, being guided on and off set by floor assistants, with mics being cabled up and connected, props brought on set as necessary, and make-up artists doing final checks. There will be a lot of movement on the studio floor – and yet as the presenter you are expected to carry on delivering the script to the viewer, keep looking to camera, and talk as if nothing else is happening 'off camera'.

Studios are soundproofed, with the director and production team in a space separate from the cameras and on-screen talent, which is usually known as a gallery or production control room. This production area could be adjacent to the studio, or on the floor above or even in a Portakabin outside the studio. Production teams, including those who are not on the studio floor, use a talkback system to communicate with each other, which explains why so many of the team outside the gallery itself wear headphones or earpieces. Hopefully they are receiving instructions – not listening to their own music systems!

Presenters use in-ear talkback to receive instructions from the director, producer and production assistant, which can be instead of, or as well as, a floor manager giving visual directions. The amount of production chat across the air-waves can be very alarming to the newcomer. On some productions, the lighting director and sound supervisor will have their own control rooms, each communicating with the main control room via talkback, which can result in even more chat over the airways – when I worked at the main BBC Television Centre in White City some of the technical team were in the basement, so they too were on talkback in another part of the building. Presenters in stu-dios learn to distinguish what instructions they need to listen to! There is more on this in the section on page 94: 'How to work with in-ear talkback'.

On simple location recordings the presenter is unlikely to use in-ear talkback – unless they are in a live, two-way con-versation with the main studio – as the location director will usually be in line of sight of the presenter to give verbal or visual instructions. If the director is out of sight or earshot, another member of the production team can cue the presenter, or walkie-talkies could be used.

Studio programmes can be shot in front of live audiences. There may be raked audience seating with the audience in front of the presenter, such as BBC's *Have I Got News for You?* The audience could surround the set, as in ITV's *Dancing on Ice*, or they could be standing in the set and very close to the presenters, as on BBC's *Top Gear*.

It is great fun working to a live studio audience, and you may be tempted to address them because they are physically in the studio with you. Study presenters on television pro-grammes that use an audience: there will be exceptions when the presenter looks directly at the live audience for a reaction, particularly in a chat-show format, but on the whole you will find that talking to the camera takes precedence.

You might find yourself on a location shoot with audiences or crowds of onlookers – and again the same basic rules apply. However, a camera crew on location also attracts crowds who may not have been invited, and passers-by who sometimes try and get on camera. The production team may be large enough to include crowd control, floor assistants and runners who will try to keep the general public out of shot, but it can be yet another distraction to deal with when out of the controlled studio environment.

Studio shoots are extremely expensive to run, sometimes hundreds of thousands of pounds an hour, so time really is money. Generally speaking, most studio shows make use of a prompting device, such as Autocue or Autoscript, so presenters can read the script rather than speak from memory; it is quicker for the presenter to read the links than go for several takes if they forget their lines.

Whether in a studio or on location, you will still need focus and concentration to cope with the different demands of each environment.

66 I enjoy both. Working on location is always fun. When doing vox pops, you can meet some great people! Sometimes the weather and surroundings can be tough, so you have to learn to be adaptable.

Seema Pathan, presenter,
Price-drop TV, Bid TV, The Business Channel

## How to present live and recorded programmes

Whether it's multi-camera or single camera, studio, location or OB, the shoot could be live or recorded.

❝ Live TV is always challenging because there is no safety net. There is more pressure with live TV and if you get something wrong it still gets shown. Recorded is more forgiving as you can retake.

Denise Ching, guest presenter, QVC

There are pros and cons to working on both live and recorded TV. Some presenters and production teams love the live experience. There's the rush of adrenaline when you are on air, and when it's over, that's it, all go home. If there were mistakes, well of course these should be investigated, and lessons will be learned, but there's little you can do about it once the transmission is over. Live programmes can be found throughout the schedule, including news and current affairs, shopping channels, sport, concerts and events, some children's programmes, a few chat shows. Live means that as you speak to camera your words and on-screen picture are being transmitted simultaneously, although some programmes do have a built-in time delay of a few seconds for editorial or censorship reasons.

Presenting live requires the ability to think on your feet, preparation for the unexpected, and nerves of steel until you get used to it. Interviewees who are chatty in rehearsal can become too nervous to speak on camera; guests, celebrities, children and animals can be unpredictable; and technical failure can strike at any time. How you cope with the situation depends on the type of programme and whether it is acceptable to reveal to the viewer that something has gone wrong. It is not only your responsibility – a good director will give instructions via talkback or the floor manager to guide you to plan B!

Pre-recorded programmes can be made months, weeks, days or hours before transmission. They could be recorded as several separate sequences to be edited together, or recorded 'as live' without pausing for retakes. Some programmes which seem to be live are actually pre-recorded, such as ITV's *Who Wants to be a Millionaire?*, recorded a few days ahead, and BBC's *Question Time*, pre-recorded just hours before transmission.

66 Recorded TV takes more time as you are going back to review the recording, re-recording segments and working on getting things perfect. With a live recording, it is what it is; once it's done it is out there. Live recording time seems to fly by and before you know it you're getting the signal that you've got 'X' minutes to wrap up.

Marilyn Devonish, presenter, *The Life Success Show* (Sky)

Although it might seem at first glance that to work on pre-recorded programmes would be less stressful, it is not always the case. There are often too many opportunities to go for another take and to improve on what you have already recorded. An inexperienced director might ask for several more takes than are really necessary – if the programme had been live, take one would have been transmitted and that would be the end of it!

Too many retakes can have a detrimental effect. As a director over the years, I have sat in edit suites on countless productions selecting the best takes. Although it may have seemed like a good idea at the time to record several takes, very often we would use the first or second one even if they were not perfect, because the earlier takes had a better energy. As a presenter, you should try to make every take as good as it can be, and try not to run out of steam. It can be reassuring to work on recorded programmes, to feel that if you make a mistake you can ask to do it again, but you cannot rely on that. The schedule may not allow for multiple retakes, and there is no substitute for learning your lines and being professional.

66 Live really has you on your toes! It fills you with adrenaline and you really do have to make sure your preparations have been done. It's unpredictable too: what worked in rehearsal doesn't always work in transmission, things go wrong, and you have to be sharp and adjust throughout. Recording is different. You have an awareness that if you get it wrong you can start over. The challenge is sometimes to make take eight as engaging as take one or two. My preferred format is live-to-tape recording. Rehearse a little, then do one take, and you tend get that raw energy or enthusiasm for the topic or idea from your guest that additional recording can lose.

Michael O'Donoghue, Higher Education producer/manager;
presenter, Distance Learning TV

## How to walk and talk

Whether you are presenting on live or recorded TV, it won't always be from a stationary or seated position, you may be required to walk and talk – at the same time!

Most of you will have been walking and talking since you were about two years old, but sometimes when asked to walk and talk to camera, presenters either forget their words or can't put one foot in front of the other. Yet walking and talking simultaneously is something presenters are frequently asked to do, whether in a studio or on location. In fact, some presenters find it easier to walk and talk than to deliver a script from a seated or standing position, as walking makes things seem more natural, gives you something to do with your arms, and can release more energy.

Here are some pointers:

- Know your words thoroughly: it's amazing how a word-perfect but stationary rehearsal can become a muddle when on the move.
- Walk at a steady pace, not too fast and not too slowly – the camera operator or director should let you know

how it looks. If you are asked to speed up your walking pace, don't automatically start speaking more quickly, and vice versa – be able to separate the two tasks!

• Remember that if you sway your shoulders when you walk it can look ugly on a small screen, and you could veer out of shot.

The camera could be handheld, or on a tripod, a crane or a fixed high position – or even on a moving jib. You will be instructed as to what kind of move is expected from you. Find the lens and keep your eyeline to it, no matter how far away the camera seems. The camera operator could be using a long lens and be framed up on your head and shoulders, even if the camera is at the end of the street. A good tip is to take one or two steps before you start to speak, so that the shot does not start with you talking right at the beginning. This will give the editor a chance to mix to this shot from the previous one, and also gives you a chance to get into the flow.

As a general rule, if the camera operator is walking backwards and you are walking forwards, keep a constant distance between you so that you remain in focus and in frame. If you stop walking, the camera operator will stop, so do not stop and start without warning or you may risk a collision! You could be asked to walk and then stop at an agreed point in the script, or stop on a marked position.

How do you stop on a prearranged mark without making it look obvious? You can line up the mark with an object you can see out of the corner of your eye, such as a tree, and judge when you have reached the point. Or, in rehearsal, walk from the agreed end point back towards the start whilst saying your script, and you will find out exactly where to start walking and speaking from. An alternative beginning to the shot is when the camera operator starts on another object or view and moves the camera to find you already speaking. You will need to know when to start speaking, and you will be given a cue by the director or camera operator. Usually you can sense when the camera lens is on you. An alternative ending is to walk past camera, out of shot at the end of the piece, which looks good if you smile just before you leave frame.

Whether you are in a field or a stadium, in a swimming pool, halfway up a mountain, or in a busy high street, keep concentrating and maintain your eyeline to camera. There will be no need to shout (except if there is background noise) because the sound recordist will pick up your voice wherever the camera is.

Walking-and-talking shots on location are unlikely to use a prompt, but in a studio you could be walking from one part of the set to another whilst reading from a prompt. Don't let your audition be your first encounter with a prompt.

### How to read from a prompt without looking like you are reading

66 You have to always remember to make it expressive and not show you are reading!

Jill Kenton, presenter, jnetradio.com, Hayes FM, QVC, *Dress My Mate*; contributor, *BBC Breakfast*

Newscasters 'read' the news to the viewer. Presenters can deliver hours of written material, live or recorded, without referring to a script. What is the technique of reading from a prompt without looking as if you are actually reading? Prompting devices such as Autocue, Autoscript or Portaprompt scroll the script on a screen in front of the camera lens for the presenter to read without the words being visible to the viewer at home. It's all done with mirrors! The system is usually controlled by an operator who adjusts the speed. It is also possible in some situations, such as in a regional newsroom, for the presenter to self-operate.

The trick to using a prompting device is that you should deliver the script as if you are talking to the viewer, not reading to the viewer. The TV audience should not really notice whether you are ad libbing, working from cue cards, delivering a script from memory or reading the script from a prompt – it should all be delivered in a conversational way. When the viewer is aware that you are 'reading', it will get in the way of the 'performance' and they will feel alienated because you will have stopped talking naturally to them.

When reading from a prompt it is particularly important to vary the vocal delivery, to pause when necessary, and to breathe. Try pausing when you see a comma, and a full stop means stop! Reading aloud is something we rarely do in everyday life, unless reading a bedtime story to a child, but this skill is invaluable for presenting.

**“** A prompting device is essential for a news programme where there are lots of serious news links one after another, but in my experience, it's best not to script interviews or fun little sections as they will usually come across as too contrived.

Becky Jago, presenter, *Anglia Tonight*, *Newsround*,
*Sky Sports News*, GMTV's *Entertainment Today*

Try studying live, 'on the sofa' chat shows, and observe how the presenters use a prompt for most of the scripted content, then move seamlessly from reading to chatting with their co-presenter, or interviewing a guest, and then back to the prompt. If their performance is professional and slick the viewer should not be aware which sections are being read.

The prompt screen looks very much like a computer screen. The script is typed on a computer and can be displayed in a variety of typefaces and font sizes. It can be modified to be bold, underlined, italic, inverse, with black or different coloured backgrounds. The fonts can be mixed to suit short-sighted or long-sighted readers.

If you are a short-sighted presenter co-hosting with a long-sighted presenter, your individual scripts can be displayed in different-sized fonts. You can also vary the combination of foreground and background colours which can make it easier for people who find sight-reading difficult. You can personalise the settings to suit you, but a word of warning – the screen size is fixed. If the font is too big then fewer words will be visible on the screen at once, so it may be harder to view enough words to make sense of the sentence.

One of the most common worries is that the prompt will go too fast – don't panic, you are in control because you are setting the pace. The prompt operator's job is to follow your pace, and if they go too slowly or too quickly they may not be rehired! If you speak quickly, the prompt will go quickly to match your speed, and if you speak slowly, the prompt will go slowly. If you stop to have an ad-lib chat with your co-host, the prompt will stop and when you return to the script, the prompt will start scrolling again.

Just to reinforce the point – what will you do if the prompt is going too quickly? Speed up or slow down? The correct answer is to slow down! If the prompt is going too quickly it is most likely that you are reading too quickly; the worst thing to do is to read more quickly to catch up, as that will make it go even faster, and it will become like a runaway train – you may never catch up with it!

The prompt screen has a cursor which is usually about one third down from the top on the left-hand side. This is where your eyeline should be, and in a professional studio it will be lined up with the lens, so you will automatically be looking directly at the viewer. The operator will line up the words to the cursor, raising them up to your eyeline as you read, so that you do not need to scan the screen too much. If the camera is placed at the correct distance from the presenter, the viewer will not notice the small movements of the eyes as you read.

If possible, check your hard copy of the script beforehand so you can spot any errors. As the script and the prompt come from the same source, any mistakes will be on both – so check for spelling mistakes, over-long sentences or tricky phrases, and correct them before you are on air, rather than when you are actually broadcasting. Many presenters highlight, underline, capitalise or use bold type for key words in the sentences to help read them with correct emphasis. You can add simple camera and stage directions on the prompt such as 'Turn to camera 3', 'Interview next' or 'Smile'!

If you are using a prompt in a live programme, keep your hard copy up to date. As you read one story, put it to the back of the pile so that if the prompt fails on item ten and you look down to read from your script, you will continue to read the correct story, not be faced with item one. Observe how professional newscasters discreetly keep their scripts in order.

❝ A prompt is the presenter's equivalent of a comfort blanket, but as ever, technology isn't infallible so always be prepared for things to go wrong! That way, if they do, you'll always have a back-up plan and won't panic. Always have an ad lib up your sleeve.

Nicci Brighten, presenter,
*Love Your Home Show*, 2008, Radio Wey 87.9 FM

If you are using a prompt at an event and it is not appropriate to hold a script in vision, know the script thoroughly, or have some standby cards. Known as cue cards, these are the size of large postcards that you can hold in your hand, featuring key information as bullet points that you could use to jog your memory.

How can you practise at home without a prompting device? Reading aloud is very useful, and something we don't tend to do apart from storytelling. Some websites allow you to practise by using a type of prompting software on your computer. The Resources section in the Appendix has more details.

Many people make the mistake of wanting to start their presenter training with reading from a prompt. I feel it is important to establish a relationship with the viewer first. Remember that the camera is behind the words on the prompt, so talk to the viewer. Don't just read the words but try to look 'through' the words to the lens.

The 'Reading from a Prompt' self-assessment checklist (see page 197) gives the main points to bear in mind when reading from a prompt. You can photocopy it and use it to chart your progress.

66 I believe I am more natural using my own words rather than reading from a prompt. However, sometimes you can get tongue-tied or if you are ever in a situation where you don't know what to say, the prompt can be a saviour!

Seema Pathan, presenter,
Price-drop TV, Bid TV, The Business Channel

As well as using prompting systems presenters frequently use in-ear talkback. Again don't let your screen test be the first time you come across this device.

## How to work with in-ear talkback

66 Have you ever thought you were hearing voices inside your head? Well, for a TV presenter this is the reality. But don't worry because you're not going crazy. It's all part of the job of using in-ear talkback. To do it well you need to be good at multitasking and be able to split your attention from that little voice in your ear giving you instructions and what you are projecting to the viewers.

Nicci Brighten, presenter,
*Love Your Home Show*, 2008, Radio Wey 87.9 FM

You've probably seen presenters wearing an earpiece, which is sometimes more visible than it should be! Have you ever thought about why an earpiece is necessary, and more importantly, what it feels like to have someone talking in your ear at the same time as you are speaking?

In-ear talkback is a system that allows people to talk directly to the presenter without the person giving instructions being seen or heard by the viewers. It's usually the producer, director or production assistant who will talk to the presenter, though hopefully not at the same time!

It consists of an earpiece that fits just inside the ear, held in place with a piece of curved plastic behind the ear and a collar clip or tape on the back of the neck. Coiled tubing connects the earpiece to a receiver pack that is placed out of sight in the presenter's back pocket or taped to their clothing. The earpiece and coiled tubing are usually hidden by long hairstyles, but can be visible when worn by presenters with short hair.

The sound assistant will provide you with the whole device. The earpiece itself can be given a hygienic wipe between users, or the top section that fits inside the ear can be replaced with each use. One of the problems with using an earpiece is that ear shapes differ widely from one person to another, and if you are unlucky the earpiece can fall out during a live transmission. You can get round this by having your own earpiece moulded to fit your ear – and then take it with you from job to job, confident that it will not have been used by anyone else and that it will not fall out. (For information on where to obtain your own earpiece see the Resources in the Appendix). There is a volume control on the talkback device, which you should check and adjust before recordings or transmission, but make sure you don't turn it down too much or you may miss vital commands or start fiddling with the volume in shot.

As previously mentioned, in a typical TV studio the production teams use talkback to communicate with each other. Camera operators, floor managers, floor assistants and runners wear headphones or in-ear talkback devices to communicate with the control rooms; the presenter is no exception and is included in this system. You will need to know things like how much time you have left on the interview, how many seconds there are to the commercial break or end of the programme, that the next link is to camera two, or that the interviewee is running late and you will need to 'fill' for thirty seconds. Some of these instructions could be conveyed through the floor manager, but talkback is more direct. The producer might want to feed you some information, such as a particular question to ask, while the interview is actually taking place, and the most practical way to get this information to you is by talkback.

There are two main types of talkback system: 'open' or 'closed', the latter also known as 'switched' or 'keyed'. In open talkback, the presenter can hear everything that is being said in the control room, whether it is intended for the presenter to hear or not. It could include the director speaking to the cameras, the production assistant calling the shots, or just miscellaneous chat about what people did last night, and what time the meal break is scheduled for. In amongst this chat there will be instructions for the presenter, such as 'Slow down, you're speaking too fast.' The presenter has to filter out what is relevant to them, and what is not. Hopefully the person speaking to the presenter will say the presenter's name before the instruction, to alert them to listen out, but that doesn't always happen.

If closed, switched or keyed talkback is used, the person giving instructions to the presenter will press a switch or key in the control room before speaking, and the presenter will hear only what is said whilst the switch is depressed. At the end of the instruction when the switch is turned off, the presenter will not hear anything more from the control room until the switch is pressed again.

Some presenters prefer open talkback as they can hear everything that is going on in the control room, and they feel in touch with events – or disasters – as they unfold! In this case, it is really important to filter out what is not relevant to you. Other presenters only want to know what is meant for them, and do not want to be distracted by production chat. It is possible to mix the two types of talkback, depending on the production and the studio facilities. In some productions, both open and closed talkback are used on the same programme, but for different purposes and for different presenters. Sometimes the presenter may not have a choice, as some control rooms are wired for a certain type of communication, but it is worth knowing that these two main types of talkback exist, so that you do not get taken by surprise.

**66** Some people find talkback very frustrating and off-putting and will choose to have keyed talkback. I prefer to know everything that's going on up in the gallery. Sometimes it gets a little loud and can be off-putting, but that's usually because of some late-breaking news or change in the order of the programme. If you trust that your director will tell you directly what you need to know, you can almost blur out the rest of it!

Becky Jago, presenter, *Anglia Tonight, Newsround, Sky Sports News*, GMTV's *Entertainment Today*

One presenter I know was in an audition using an earpiece, and she was not aware that closed talkback was being used. As she wasn't hearing any instructions from the control room, she assumed (wrongly) that the talkback was defective, so she made up her own instructions. Then she heard a voice in her ear! Talkback was working, but it was closed talkback, and the production team hadn't told her. She was totally thrown by this, and it interfered badly with her performance.

Talkback and earpieces are not restricted to the studio. Supposing you are the presenter on location – you could be in a variety of situations from a war zone to an arts festival. The main studio will link to you for your report, and may want to ask you further questions on air. Your earpiece is your way of hearing the studio anchor, or host, who will hand over to you and have a two-way conversation.

How do you use talkback without looking distracted? Think of all the multitasking you do every day. Do you watch TV while typing on your laptop at the same time as conducting a conversation with someone and also eating a snack? Do you answer the phone and chat while continuing to listen to a radio play? Without realising it, you are probably already homing in on the most significant speaker while letting the others drift into the background. That is the same set of skills required for listening to in-ear talkback – learn to select what's important and ignore the rest.

Unlike real life, when you are presenting and receiving instructions via talkback, you *can't* talk back! You must be able to receive information but not reveal that you are being spoken to – your guests, interviewees and viewers must not realise you are listening to a voice in your ear. Like so many areas of TV presenting, you need to split your mind in two so that you carry on presenting but also absorb whatever is being told to you. It could be anything from 'Your earpiece is showing, pull your hair over your ear' to 'Late-breaking news story coming in, stand-by for a news flash.' Hopefully the speaker will not be rude or shout in your ear – there's nothing worse – but whatever the tone, do not react with an inappropriate expression on your face.

The best way to practise working with in-ear talkback, if you do not have access to one, is to ask someone to give instructions to you while you are speaking. Prepare a script to deliver to camera, and while you are speaking get a friend to feed you information. They could count you down from ten seconds to zero, or as you conduct an interview they could suggest questions to ask.

It is worth remembering that some productions also use a floor manager to give hand signals to the presenter, or cue cards with pre-written instructions. In either case, liaise with the floor manager beforehand, know what the signals mean, and when presenting just glance at them out of the corner of your eye. A good floor manager will be in your eyeline so that you do not need to take your gaze away from the guest or camera.

What is it actually like to work with in-ear talkback?

66 Talkback at first is really strange; however, once you get used to it, you feel lost with out it! You need to be able to listen to direction whilst presenting, which comes with time. Also you need to be able to block out information that is not relevant to you and absorb and take on board the information that is.

Seema Pathan, presenter,
Price-drop TV, Bid TV, The Business Channel

66 Trying to listen to your guest and trying to work out if the producer is talking to you or not in your ear is even harder than trying to rub your tummy and pat your head!

Charlie Lemmer, presenter,
Real Estate Channel, Dubai Eye, Abu Dhabi TV, Current TV

## How to interview

66 Allow the guest the maximum time to speak, listen well to steer the interview with relevant questions, also connect with the guest to make them feel comfortable.

Renée Castle, presenter, Caribbean New Media Group,
Caribbean Communications Network,
Sun Community Television

Interviews can range from cosy to confrontational, political to personal, from a two-minute chat to the twelve-day Frost/Nixon marathon, but there is some common ground for all interview styles. Your role as interviewer is to ask the questions the viewers would like to ask. If something needs further explanation, pose the questions you feel the viewers would want answered.

Programmes differ, of course: on some productions you may be required to do your own background research; on others there could be a team of researchers providing you with information. In both situations, be prepared in advance by finding out as much as possible about the guest and the topic. Always have more notes and questions than you actually need, in case the guest is less chatty than expected.

66 The only disaster would be when, during an interview, the guest doesn't talk – just learn to fill and fill and fill! Remember they are not professional and can get shy at the worst of times!

Jill Kenton, presenter, jnetradio.com, Hayes FM, QVC, *Dress My Mate*; contributor, *BBC Breakfast*

Tom Cruise famously cracked up laughing in an interview with David Letterman, and Meg Ryan was notoriously difficult and monosyllabic during an interview with Michael Parkinson, so it can be unpredictable. You should discuss the aim of the interview with the production team beforehand, and during the course of the conversation try to shape it to have a successful outcome. Some guests have their own agenda; they may want to talk about their new book, whereas you may want them to reveal all about their recent divorce. If you do not subtly take control you could find you've run out of time, irritated the producer, and all the viewer has heard is a shameless plug!

It is usual for the interviewer to discuss, in advance, with the interviewee what ground the interview will cover. Interviews are not usually rehearsed in full, or they can lose spontaneity, but the interviewee may want to know what answers to prepare. Generally it is best to give the gist of the questioning, rather than each specific question. Some interviewees, or their managers, will want to veto the questions in advance; some interviewers will want to surprise their guests with a line of questioning. It's all down to context.

Introduce yourself to the interviewee before the recording to check how they would like to be addressed – Sir John Jones, Sir John, John Jones, or Johnnie? Confirm the basics, as researchers have been known to get background facts wrong. Be aware of any subject the guest doesn't want to be interviewed about, but bear in mind the difference between current affairs and daytime chat show, as the role of the current-affairs interviewer can often involve trying to get answers on thorny topics, whereas the daytime chat-show interview should be more relaxed.

Think about the phrasing of your questions; closed questions such as 'How many people were involved?' or 'Was it a success?' might elicit a one-word answer, whereas open questions such as 'Do you feel there were enough people involved?' or 'What made it successful?' should produce a longer response. You might want the answer to be one word, or you might be looking for a deeper explanation, so consider your questioning style and what is appropriate for the context.

A surprisingly large amount of information can be packed into a two- or three-minute interview. If the interview is short, keep the questioning style direct and simple, to maximise the amount of time you can give to the interviewee. Complex and meandering questions can cause confusion, with the interviewee not knowing which part to answer first. I am constantly impressed by Radio 4's *Today* programme, in which each day an important interview starts approximately two or three minutes before the end of the programme, covers a lot of ground, and still ends on time.

An interviewer is not just there to ask questions – the skilful interviewer is a good listener. If you relentlessly make your way down a list of questions, the interview will not be a natural conversation, and you could miss opportunities to ask supplementary questions – or worse, ask a question that has already been covered.

❝ When I first started interviewing I used to list my questions and then just work my way through them. I soon learnt that it was best to listen actively and to react to what was being said with any follow-up questions.

Becky Jago, presenter, *Anglia Tonight*, *Newsround*,
*Sky Sports News*, GMTV's *Entertainment Today*

In my view, the single most important point for an interviewer to bear in mind is to listen to the guest.

❝ Someone who not only talks but listens makes a good interviewer. Sometimes presenters are so preoccupied with asking the rehearsed questions that they don't actually listen to what the interviewee is saying and can miss opportunities to ask questions related to their answers or can ask a question that was previously answered! In this instance, it's always the presenter that comes out looking bad!

Gemma Hunt, presenter, *Barney's Barrier Reef*,
*Xchange* (CBBC); guest co-presenter, *Smile*

Have the confidence to acknowledge the answers and create bridges to the next question. If an answer is convoluted you could summarise it for the viewer, and then link to the next question.

Think about the beginning. How do you want to introduce your guest/s? Are they in vision during the intro or are they revealed after? You could use the intro to put across concisely some background facts, which frees up time in the interview for the more personal and emotional answers. These decisions may have already been made by the production team, but be aware of these points and know what you would do if asked.

Have a plan for the ending, and make sure you finish the interview on time. The classic mistake made by new presenters is to panic and start to wrap up the interview too early, which can leave an embarrassingly long amount of time to actually say goodbye. If you needed to, you could say 'thanks and goodbye' very swiftly – try timing yourself to see how long it takes. For inspiration, study live television and radio to see how professional presenters wind up interviews. Again, I recommend Radio 4's *Today* programme to hear how their presenters bring the interview to a close just before the 9 a.m. pips. It can take years to become an accomplished interviewer, and it does get easier with practice, but journalism skills are certainly very useful (for some resources on journalism, see the Appendix).

What do other professional presenters feel makes a good interviewer?

66 The interviewee is probably nervous. The interview is about them not you, so you need to do everything you can to enable them to say what they need to say.

Cate Conway, presenter, *The Seven Thirty Show* (UTV),
*Cooking in the Community* (Northern Visions)

## How to do vox pops

An interview is an extended, prearranged chat with a guest, whereas a vox pop is a quick, off-the-cuff response from a passer-by.

Vox pops, 'the voice of the people', can crop up in a range of programmes, from news to children's, on topics as diverse as 'What do you think of the economy at the moment?' to 'What's your favourite kind of birthday party?' They can form a useful comment from any section of society, a quick video straw poll. Vox pops can be shot with a minimal crew, usually a reporter/presenter and a camera/sound operator, and they are often filmed in the street or shopping centres, where there are usually plenty of willing participants.

The kinds of questions that work best are ones that don't need too much thinking about, that are not too personal, and that elicit interesting or comical answers. The editor will take the best ones and cut them together to make a short, snappy item, which is normally one or two minutes in duration.

It takes confidence to approach strangers in the street and ask them questions on camera. Be friendly and polite, avoid being overly 'touchy-feely', steer clear of topics that could cause offence, and smile! Do not take it personally if the passer-by does not want to answer; after all, how would you like it if a camera and mic were thrust into your face? On the whole, people will not come to you, you will need to approach them, so pick a crowded place.

The camera operator will appreciate it if you identify who you are going to ask before you actually walk up to them, so that he or she can frame up. If you are only using one mic, remember to hold it under the mouth of the person who is speaking. Position yourself so you and the speaker are both in shot, or allow the cameraman to find a good head-and-shoulders shot of the speaker. It works well if the shots are a mixture of people facing right and facing left, so when it is all edited together they are not all facing in the same direction. Don't look at your notes when asking questions or the speaker's eyeline may be directed to your notepad rather than your face.

You need more answers than you think to get a reasonable number of useable ones, as some responses might be uninteresting or controversial (and therefore unbroadcastable), so do allow enough shooting time. Vox pops can be great fun, and if you choose a question that is successful, they can make entertaining items for showreels. Some general tried and tested ones are 'When was the last time you cooked for your partner, and what did you cook?', 'If you could go anywhere in the world tomorrow, where would you go and why?', 'If you won a million pounds, what would you do with the money?', 'What would you save if your house was burning down?', 'When was the last time you had a hug?' and 'What do you look for in a potential partner?' Make a list of possible questions you could ask.

Try going out in a busy street with a friend operating a video camera or phone and have a go. Bear in mind that some areas and shopping centres will require you to ask for permission before you start filming.

When you review your footage, the main points to look out for are: did you allow the interviewee to speak or did you talk over them? And do you have enough good 'soundbite' answers that can be edited together to make an interesting sequence?

So far we've been looking at generic presenting techniques, but the following sections explore some specialised genres.

## How to present on shopping channels

Shopping channels are a great source of work for presenters. Currently there are around forty shopping channels available on Sky, and scores more online shopping channels covering many diverse areas: travel, lifestyle, DIY, home, jewellery, cookery and sports. Some people underestimate the skills involved in shopping-channel presenting, as well as the considerable rewards: it is possible to earn hundreds of pounds per hour as a presenter on one of the mainstream shopping channels.

The presenting skills required are not for the faint-hearted – live and unrehearsed talking to camera, to time, without a script or prompt, simultaneously acting on instructions received via talkback, interviewing experts and handling props in the form of items for sale. Depending on the channel you may also need to react to changing information, such as the quantity still available or a price drop, and read details off a monitor with viewer feedback on the product. You might work late shifts, as shopping channels can be live on air round the clock, seven days per week.

Some channels use a product buyer or producer to inform the presenters, others ask you to create your own brief to outline the key features of the product. The viewer will need to know: what is the product, what does it do, what is it made of, how does it work, the size, weight, dimensions, and the unique selling points. In other words, research the product and know it well enough to be able to chat about it fluently for as long as required. The main features of the product can be written as bullet points on cards (kept out of vision) for you to glance at when appropriate. You will need to assimilate a lot of facts quickly and be able to convey those key points expertly to the viewer without sounding hesitant or unnatural.

The ability to structure what you are talking about is paramount – you will not be working from a formal script, so you will need to create a good beginning, middle and ending. Of course, there will be a house style, but no one will be actually telling you exactly what to say and when, so you will need to use your initiative. The key features should be mentioned right at the start of your presentation, followed by your personal comments to show how you connect with the product. The ending might be a recap of the main features, plus a reminder of the price and how to purchase.

Handling props on television is slightly different to handling objects in your day-to-day life. Move the product more slowly to help the camera operators to keep it framed and in focus, and keep it still for long enough so that the director can get close-ups. Show the product to the viewer, not to yourself, which might mean it is the wrong way round to you. Take care not to mask the product with your hands, and know where the close-up cameras are placed.

Have a look at the different styles of shopping channels and programmes. Some, like Price-drop TV, use one presenter at a time in a hard sell against the clock. Others like QVC use a presenter and an expert who chat about the product in a more conversational way. Common to both is the ability to describe the product in great detail, almost as if on radio, telling viewers what you see, feel, smell, taste and hear.

Del Brown is a live studio director and vision mixer at QVC, was launch director and vision mixer at Express Shopping Channel, and launch director, vision mixer and senior producer at Challenge Jackpot. He feels:

**66** It is the presenter's main role to push, drive and encourage sales and to make sure the presentation explains the product's key features and benefits clearly to the viewers. If there is a guest linked to the products, the presenter's role is to try and extract the best out of them. The presenter is also the friendly face of the channel.

Del also explains how much talkback a typical shopping-channel presenter will have to deal with:

**66** Shopping-channel presenters are usually on open talkback so they can hear the director calling the shots, speaking to the floor, the camera operators, the graphics operator, etc. They can also hear the producer talking to the floor, to the director, and giving sales updates to the presenter. Presenters will be expected to talk to the right camera, turn in vision between cameras when prompted, hold things steady when cameras are getting close-ups. The producer will instruct the presenter to give key points during the presentation which they will have to seamlessly integrate into what they are saying. The director will be counting the presenter to start and stop talking. Presenters will be expected to stop talking at 'zero' and not overrun, as that will have knock-on effects to the rest of the broadcast.

Co-presenters, experts or guests can appear for a section of the programme to explain the product; they can be from retail or manufacturing backgrounds, or actors with experience of demonstrating products. They might receive in-ear instructions on timings, and be included in directions from the producer to the presenter prompting specific questions, such as 'How many batteries does the product require?', so they can get an answer ready.

Apart from the above technical skills and personal style, the ability to connect with the product is one of the most important qualities for shopping-channel presenting. Use the product, find a way of making it come alive, so that it is not just an object that you are trying to sell. Finally, shopping channels take personal grooming seriously – pay attention to your clothes, image, hair, make-up and especially your nails as they will probably be seen in close-up.

Some shopping channels, such as QVC, run competitions to find new presenters, which are certainly worth looking out for, and if you are not successful in gaining a presenter job you can be considered for the role of expert or guest.

66 What makes a good shopping-channel presenter is what makes a good human being – someone intelligent, someone you can trust and want to spend time with. Being real and being yourself is extremely important, not acting at being a presenter. Interest in shopping is always a help! As for what makes a good guest – it's the same as being a presenter! Product knowledge is essential, being able to talk and demonstrate, creativity, and ability to prioritise.

Barbara Gainsley, Presenter Liaison, QVC

66 One of the key skills I think a professional and successful shopping-channel presenter should possess is being able to ad lib. Shopping channels are not scripted or rehearsed and do not use Autocue. I regularly work with shopping-channel presenters who have been doing this stuff for years, but even now are not able to actually make sense whilst ad libbing. Also required is the skill to be able to work well with talkback. When things are going wrong in the gallery, presenters should be able to continue to hold the show together, whilst at the same time realising what is going wrong and remaining calm. They should be able to think on their feet and come across as warm and personable on air. Successful presenters prep their products well and take the time to find out all the details of how a product works, or some interesting background or history to the product or the company.

Del Brown, Live Director and Vision Mixer,
QVC, Express Shopping Channel, Challenge Jackpot

There is further information on what to expect in a shopping-channel audition, and what kind of training would be helpful for a shopping channel presenter in the later section on auditions and training.

## How to be a children's presenter

Like any genre you are aiming for, you need to know your market; within children's programmes there is a huge range from preschool to teenage and young adult. Does your knowledge begin and end with *Blue Peter*, or are you aware of the differences between CBBC and CBeebies, Disney Channel and Playhouse Disney, Nickelodeon and Nick Jr, Pop and Tiny Pop? Are you familiar with programmes such as *Richard Hammond's Blast Lab*, *Scorpion Island*, *Milkshake*, *The Roly Mo Show*, *Kenny the Shark*, *Backyard Science*, or characters Bella and Fizz, Dick and Dom, Oucho and Mr Tumble?

When presenters tell me they want to be a children's presenter, nine times out of ten they want to present *Blue Peter*. There's nothing wrong with that aspiration – after all, *Blue Peter* has been made by the BBC since 1958 and is one of the most well-known children's programmes across the globe. I suggest they also look at other less mainstream profile channels and programmes, such as Discovery Kids online children's channel or British Forces Broadcasting Service (BFBS), which features a children's make-and-do show, *Finger Tips*, and that they consider presenting children's radio as a way in.

The BBC started transmitting regular programmes specifically for children in the late 1940s. Some of the longest running, apart from *Blue Peter*, include storytelling *Jackanory* from 1965 to 1996, and daily news bulletins for children, like *Newsround* (established in 1972 as *John Craven's Newsround*). A BBC children's favourite from 1964 to 1988, *Playschool*, developed into *Playbus* then *Playdays*, and relaunched as *Tikkabilla* on CBeebies. The new format has many similarities to the original *Playschool*, featuring two presenters who are more mature than teenage, songs, storytelling, rhymes and enacted stories, as well as windows to the outside world (location inserts on video to show items from the real world).

Justin Fletcher is a specialist children's presenter who was awarded an MBE in 2008 for his services to children's broadcasting. Justin's credits include *Fun Song Factory*, BBC's *Tweenies, Tikkabilla* and *Something Special*, which uses Makaton sign language and for which he received a BAFTA. What attracted Justin to children's presenting, and what qualities does he feel a children's presenter should possess?

**❝** It all started when I watched Phillip Schofield in the Children's BBC broom cupboard. I just thought, 'That's what I want to do.' Children are the best audience and I have so much fun every day. I get to dress up in funny costumes and make people laugh. What could be better then that! It's also incredibly rewarding to be involved in programmes like *Something Special*, which really help children to communicate with their friends and family.

I think you have to be warm and engaging when presenting to any age group, and with children it's important to be on the same wavelength as them. They respond well if the presenter is enjoying what he or she is doing. I was taught very early on in my career to remember the '3 Cs' of children's presenting – Clarity, Commitment and Contact. I always try to remember that advice. It has helped me a lot over the years.

Clive Duncan, who presented *Playdays*, is now Co-director at London's Academy of Live and Recorded Arts (ALRA). What does Clive suggest to keep a performance natural?

❝ My producer told me to speak to the four-year-old at home on the sofa, and that's what I always think about. It's about looking through the camera, not at it, and talking to someone who is watching you.

People attracted to children's presenting tend to have some experience of working with or entertaining children, and like being with children. Within the genre there can be different kinds of presenters to suit the different target audiences. Is it possible to define what makes a successful children's presenter? Clive Duncan feels:

❝ Any presenter who treats the audience as an equal and with respect won't go far wrong. I don't like to see presenters patronise the audience.

Children's presenter Gemma Hunt trained at the University of Bedfordshire and has presented on CBBC since 2003. Her credits include *Barney's Barrier Reef*, *Xchange*, and *Smile*. How did she break into the industry?

❝ Whilst in my third year of university, I went to a seminar on how to make a showreel with an agent who represented TV presenters. Afterwards I asked her how I could go about being represented by an agent. She took me under her wing, looked at my showreel and sent it off to some of her contacts in children's television, and the rest, as they say, is history!

Becky Jago, who also studied at the University of Bedfordshire, was a main presenter on *Newsround*. What was that like?

❝ It was a very exciting job. You went into work in the morning not knowing if you were going to be interviewing Britney Spears, talking to the Prime Minister about environmental issues, or going to a classroom of children to find out what they liked in their lunchboxes! I loved the fact that it was mostly children watching (*so* much easier to talk to...) although I do know that a large number of adults were big *Newsround* fans too. It gave me incredible travel opportunities too. In the eighteen months I was there, I followed the trail of child trafficking in West Africa, reported on the Bollywood industry from Mumbai, and broadcast from Morocco, Spain, France and Gibraltar.

Children's TV is an area that attracts presenters who are devoted and immersed in the genre; some stay in that field for their entire careers, but it is possible to move into different areas.

Becky Jago's first TV job was weather presenting for Anglia. After *Newsround*, Becky presented Capital Radio's breakfast show with Chris Tarrant and then Johnny Vaughan, reported for GMTV's *Entertainment Today* and *Sky Sports News*, and became the main presenter of *Anglia Tonight*. How easy was it for Becky to move from one area to another?

**❝** In my case it was relatively easy. I was offered a job in commercial radio in London (Capital FM) as their breakfast co-presenter and showbiz correspondent. It took me directly away from children's presenting and opened up other doors doing showbiz reporting – GMTV, E4 and BBC3.

Other famous faces and household names such as Phillip Schofield and Chris Tarrant started as children's presenters and moved to entertainment. Phillip Schofield was the first in-vision continuity announcer for Children's BBC. He moved to Saturday mornings to present six years of *Going Live*, and then, via radio and theatre, to BBC Saturday evenings with *Test the Nation*, then ITV's *This Morning*, and more recently ITV's *Dancing on Ice*. Chris Tarrant presented ITV's anarchic Saturday morning show *Tiswas* from 1974 to 1981, Capital Radio's breakfast show, television game shows and clip programmes, and is now best known for presenting ITV's *Who Wants to be a Millionaire?*

If you are going to try for children's programmes, research the world of children's TV – as with all genres there will be a lot of competition out there. Clive Duncan adds:

❝ Presenting for children's TV is a huge amount of fun – and should be experienced by all would-be presenters. It's a good training ground as you have to keep items fresh and exciting whilst messing about with sticky tape, or pudding mix and other uncontrollable things. If you can succeed in that, talking about cars or music or films is a doddle.

Alison Stewart, Executive Editor of CBeebies, has specialised in preschool children's TV as a producer, director and writer working on programmes including *Tweenies, Big Cook, Little Cook, Numberjacks, Playschool* and *Fimbles*. Alison sums up:

❝ The attributes of a good children's TV presenter differ according to the age of the target audience – obviously, a gentler and warmer approach is needed for the younger audience, while a slightly more edgy manner gets the approval of older viewers. But there are some must-haves no matter what age you're playing to...

The ability to talk not just to the camera but through the camera, making a direct relationship with the viewers.

The presenter must be able to engage with what children do – have an interest in what interests them – otherwise he or she tends to sound a bit patronising.

A sense of fun!

And one definite don't for potential presenters... don't pitch your performance to the adult viewers, or try and up-age the content. If you want to be an adult presenter, go for adult presenter jobs!

## How to do 'makes' and 'demos'

Makes and demos, the staple diet of many children's programmes, are when the presenter literally makes or demonstrates something in front of the viewer. They can crop up in a wide range of programming, including children's, arts and crafts, cookery, science, gardening, shopping or general daytime.

Makes should inspire the viewer to create, and demos should explain how a product works. There are a few golden rules about makes and demos, most of which apply to almost any situation:

Practise the make or demo all the way through before you are on air or recording. Is it visually appealing and inspiring to the viewer? Talk to the viewer, or the interviewer, and maintain eyeline with them as well as the props. Know where the close-up cameras are. You may have to work with the product facing away from you and towards the camera. Are you left- or right-handed? – it could affect which close-up camera is used. Avoid anything that is too fiddly, as your fingers may mask what you are talking about. Move props more slowly than in everyday life to allow the cameras to get a good shot – you may also be instructed to hold them still for a few seconds.

Structure the presentation and clearly lay out props in order of use, trying not to go back on yourself. Check the optimum working height – should you be standing behind a table, sitting at a desk, or on a sofa? Avoid having to bend over the product which could give you poor posture and allow hair to fall over your face. Do you need table protection, apron, gloves, or to tie your hair back? Don't present a demo or a make that is too tricky, or the viewer will not be tempted to try it out at home; instead, create finished products which look good and are achievable. If you have been asked to deliver a ten-minute presentation or a three-minute make, rehearse to that time slot. Some makes or demos are co-presented, so you may not have to do it alone, and you will have guidance from the production team. Enjoy the moment and connect with the product.

In particular for makes: check the props in advance. For example, if you are doing origami, is the paper the correct size and weight? If you are writing or drawing, does the ink or pencil show clearly enough on camera? If you need to stick products together, have you got the right glue or tape for the job? If you are decorating the make, have you got the right paint? Some makes are created from beginning to end in front of the viewer in real time, and some are shown in stages. If your make has glue or paint that needs to dry, you can have pre-prepared stages to compress time. You might also want to pre-cut or pre-stick some parts of the make so as to concentrate on the more visually interesting elements such as colouring or decorating.

When doing demonstrations, research the product. Does it have any moving parts? How is it taken apart and reassembled? How does it work? Is it noisy? Does it need batteries or a plug socket? In a cooking demo, think about the stages required to fit the demo into a shorter space of time. If mixing in a bowl, a see-through bowl is better than an opaque one so the camera can see what is inside. Be hygienic!

Alison Stewart, Executive Editor of CBeebies, says that 'unless they [the presenters] are artistically inclined, a make is often a presenter's nightmare!' Here are some tips from Alison:

**❝** If you have time, practise the make – don't believe them if they tell you it's easy!

Practise working to one camera source but angling what you do slightly towards another camera source (which would be the close-up camera).

When picking up utensils from a desktop, don't make fast moves – move slowly so a camera can pan with you in close-up if required.

If it goes wrong, make light of it! Kids' makes go wrong too!

Learn any facts or info you might need to deliver while doing the make – sometimes you're asked to change the order of what you say and do at the last minute, so it's best to be on top of what you have to say.

You definitely need clean, manicured nails!

Makes and demos can be practised at home, whether it's a new coffee grinder or some preschool craft ideas from the internet. Some children's auditions will ask for a make, and you will need to demo a product for shopping-channel auditions.

## How to be a weather presenter

They say that weather is our national obsession. Michael Fish, Bill Giles, Ulrika Johnson, Francis Wilson, Rob McElwee, Carol Kirkwood, Martyn Davies and Siân Lloyd are household names. As a weather presenter, you could be broadcasting to millions of people every day.

You do not need to be a meteorologist to be a weather presenter, although most BBC national weather presenters are trained forecasters and may be employees of the Met Office. Many regional BBC stations, Channel 4, ITV, GMTV and Sky employ individual weather presenters who may have come from a journalistic or presenting background. These companies take the data from the Met Office, but use their own graphics and presenters. So the routes to becoming a weather presenter can be through the Met Office, journalism or general presenting.

About half the weather forecasts you see on television are live, and about half are pre-recorded – it depends on the channel and the time of day. Forecasts for BBC World Service, the red-button interactive service, and many on ITV tend to be pre-recorded. Generally, weather forecasts embedded within news programmes are live as this enables a two-way conversation between the anchor and the weather presenter. The decision on pre-recorded or live can be made by the forecaster in certain situations: for example, if the weather is changing rapidly, a pre-recorded bulletin may become inaccurate very quickly, and may be replaced by a live transmission.

One of the key skills is to turn facts into a story. As a weather presenter you will be given a brief by the Met Office forecaster, and it is your job to turn that into a bulletin. This has similarities to many areas of television where you are given a brief around which you need to structure a script, complete with key points. In the case of weather presenting, you will be told the weather pattern, such as bad weather in Scotland and sunny in the South, as well as the temperatures, wind speeds, and the degree of cloud cover. You need to decide how to open the broadcast and tell the story, linking up all the areas, and finish with a summary.

David Robinson works for the Met Office in design and training. What makes a successful weather presenter in his opinion?

66 You need the skill to be able to convey complex weather details into everyday terms we all use in conversation. Sometimes the use of forecasters' technical terms such as 'systems', 'troughs' and 'occluded fronts' can make you sound knowledgeable but might add confusion to viewers. I like to hear comparison in a weather forecaster... Is it warmer or colder, wetter or drier, today than yesterday, or tomorrow than today?

When you are presenting a broadcast, think about how your viewers will be using your information and maybe tailor your presentation to suit: for example, in the morning broadcast, viewers will be thinking of the commute to work and the school run. For a Friday broadcast, viewers are thinking about weekend plans, barbecues and day trips.

Simon Keeling is a professional meteorologist and weather broadcaster who worked at GMTV from 1994 to 2000, and since 2003 has been forecasting on the BBC:

❝ There is now no need to be qualified as a meteorologist to present the weather forecast. I see non-meteorological presenters as professional communicators. It is their role to take complex scientific information and present it to the public in a form that can be understood by everyone. They must entertain and inform, be credible and have empathy with viewers' experiences of the weather.

There was a time when weather forecasters used magnetic symbols of sun, clouds and rain to stick on a map, and some even jumped from one part of the country to another on a gigantic floating map of the British Isles. Today's weather presenters use slides played in from a computer, or state-of-the-art software that creates 3D maps that fly around the screen. Most bulletins are presented in front of a chromakey screen, which inserts the weather map as a special effect, but which is invisible to the presenter. Currently, the weather bulletin on the BBC *Six O'Clock News* uses a video wall, so the presenter can actually see what is happening behind them. The job also involves multiskilling, as the presenter will be receiving instructions via in-ear talkback whilst remotely controlling the weather maps. Generally, weather presenters do not use a prompt, as the story is in their mind, and they can adapt to changing durations on air more easily if they are not reading.

An ability to talk to time is crucial – not only for live forecasts, but because so often the weather is used as a buffer in between programmes. If slides are used, then about four weather slides will make a one-minute bulletin, and the 3D map tends to have pre-programmed moves lasting about twenty to thirty seconds.

Weather forecasts are available on demand – it is possible to receive them from the Met Office direct to your mobile phone. In future, forecasts will be tailored to suit different needs; for example, for those at sea. As a weather presenter in these media you may not be on national television, but you could be seen by millions of people on their phones.

So if you can take a brief, interpret it into user-friendly language, deliver it with personality and confidence on live transmissions while using in-ear talkback and operating a remote control, then the role of weather presenter could suit you. There are some specific training courses for weather presenters (see the Resources section in the Appendix for details).

## How to present for different screens

Screens are getting bigger and smaller. Domestic televisions seem to be as large as mini cinema screens, displaying high-definition widescreen images in our lounges. Broadcast television and videos on demand are available on laptops, personal computers and mobile phones. On all sizes of screens we can view videos, live news, download short films and connect to web-presenters. As a presenter, your face and features could be viewed on a seventy-inch TV screen or a mobile phone. Does size matter?

In 1925, when John Logie Baird gave his first public demonstration of TV, the image was black and white, and grainy. Now, high-definition digital transmission enables the audience to see and review television pictures in a richness of detail never before available in our homes. During 2008–2012, analogue TV transmissions have been switched over to digital, and almost everyone should be able to receive high-quality images. Increasingly, the performer and performance are examined in excruciating detail from the comfort of our sofa – every nuance, twitch, defect, facial expression and smile. It's not only images that have become significantly larger-than-life; state-of-the-art TV speakers and digital surround-sound allows us to hear the spoken word more clearly and powerfully than previously possible.

Conversely, we can also view images from our desks and on handheld devices much closer than we would normally watch TV. Does this make us feel more connected to the presenter or will an irritating presenter become more so because of their proximity? If we were to view the same programme on a supersize, widescreen, high-definition television set, and on a tiny mobile-phone screen, would we relate to the presenter any differently?

What effect does this have on the performer? Do they have to alter their performance to fill the large screen? Should they change their style or make the performance bigger or smaller? Are there any aspects to this new technology that the presenter should be aware of? And should the presenter consider which format their programme will be viewed on?

The presenter should always relate to the camera, speak to the viewer as a one-to-one conversation, no matter what size screen or format is used by the viewer. The presenter cannot possibly predict the location and situation of the transmitted programme, especially with so many platforms and digital channels, which could show repeats for many years to come. However, it is worth bearing in mind that simplicity works best for smaller screens, that is, minimal arm and body movement, as can be seen on some web-presenting sites.

If the presenter were to make their performance bigger for the larger screens, it would be unsuitable for the small screens. Not only that, it would look phoney, over the top and insincere. So my advice is to always talk to camera as normally, naturally and simply as you can.

What does make a difference is the introduction of high definition, as it reveals tiny details of skin texture, make-up, and what's 'behind the eyes'. Make-up artists, lighting and camera operators have had to adjust their techniques for high definition, and presenters should be aware that it could allow the viewer to pick up normally imperceptible shortcomings in hair, make-up and performance.

High definition will mean scrupulous attention to personal grooming, such as manicures, teeth whitening and hair roots that need tinting. When high definition is combined with widescreen, watch out if you have any problems with your weight, as the 16 x 9 cameras for widescreen can make you look larger than you really are.

So, how do you present for different screens? There is no real difference, the core skills of presenting stay the same. But, whatever the size of screen, there will always be room for error – not everything will go according to plan.

## How to cope with on-air disasters

Murphy's Law states that 'what can go wrong will go wrong', and working in TV is no exception. Stuff will always go wrong in TV production; the trick is knowing how to deal with it when it does and having the personality to cope with disasters.

The prompt will break down, you will drop a priceless antique, forget your words, misread a script, the guest will be late, there will be costume, hair and make-up disasters, as well as snow, tears, sickness, technical failure and camera breakdown.

In my TV career I have experienced or witnessed all the above – and more. How you deal with the situation is what sets some people apart from others and gets you remembered for being a true professional.

If the prompt breaks down – immediately refer to your hard-copy script (which you should have kept up to date), use cue cards or ad lib to the next video item or commercial break.

If you drop a prop – you could send yourself up a bit for being so clumsy, apologise and carry on.

If you forget your words or misread the script – well, you are only human, apologise and carry on.

If the guest is late – fill until they arrive, either by ad libbing or going to the next guest or item. It is perfectly acceptable to candidly confess that a guest is running late or caught in traffic.

If there are costume, hair and make-up disasters – get them fixed before going for a recording or the guest or presenter may not give their best. Do not use the person responsible again.

If there is so much snow that you and the crew spend six hours getting home and then have to be back in the morning for the next day's shoot – that's tough, but who said TV was glamorous? I worked with a crew who spent the night sleeping in their cars because they could not get home, and no one missed the next day's recording.

If there are tears – give support, and go for a take when ready.

If there is sickness – well, actually most people in TV will turn up for work even if they are sent home again.

Technical failures and camera breakdowns can happen frequently – you need to think on your feet and listen out for new instructions.

Del Brown works in live daily news and shopping channels. How does he recommend that presenters cope with disasters?

❝ Firstly, remain calm despite the explosion of noise in their ears which is the panic heard from the gallery. Presenters should be able to respond quickly to instructions given in their ear. Presenters should strive to cover mistakes and not highlight them. There is nothing worse than hearing a presenter tell the audience that something has gone wrong then wait on live television for the problem to be fixed. Far better if a presenter can cover any problems whilst the gallery tries to fix it.

And here's how some professional presenters have coped when things did not go according to plan:

❝ The first time I ever presented *Newsround*, the plasma screen in the wall behind me fell down during a link. I heard the crash but didn't dare look round for fear of corpsing! Luckily it happened when I was reading an out-of-vision link so I just acted as if nothing had happened. For the rest of the programme I had two men behind me holding up this big monitor to fill a huge gap!

Becky Jago, presenter, *Anglia Tonight*, *Newsround*,
*Sky Sports News*, GMTV's *Entertainment Today*

❝ Working on a live shopping channel means that quite often mistakes and disasters happen! I was once selling an air bed and I was lying on it to demonstrate how firm and stable it was. A few minutes into the sell I stuck my heel in it and the air slowly started coming out of the bed... and it started sinking! It was very funny and I couldn't hide it so I was honest and recommended that wearing heels on an air bed was probably not a good idea!

I believe that being honest and also being able to laugh at yourself are key to presenting to allow viewers' trust and support.

Seema Pathan, presenter,
Price-drop TV, Bid TV, The Business Channel

❝ I showed up for a programme expecting an audience of approximately fifteen female pensioners, only to find they had invited thirty twelve-year-olds. All of the questions and topics I had prepared for audience discussion went out the window. I remember asking the producer halfway through if we'd even get five minutes of a show as they were really unruly and cursed a lot. Surprisingly, it turned out to be the best show of the series. The magic of TV.

Cate Conway, presenter, *The Seven Thirty Show* (UTV),
*Cooking in the Community* (Northern Visions)

**❝** There have been many times on live TV where I have had to cover or deal with an on-screen disaster. I made sure that I always had a few 'emergency back-up fillers' in the back of my mind for such occasions, where I knew I could effortlessly talk about something until the storm had passed and the show was able to run as planned!

Gemma Hunt, presenter, *Barney's Barrier Reef*,
*Xchange* (CBBC); guest co-presenter, *Smile*

**❝** I had a guest who was a specialist. All through rehearsal she was fine – very bubbly – and we worked out a framework for questions and responses that worked very well. Come the live interview, though, she just clammed up! She went pale and sat so rigid in her chair I thought she was about to faint. She was so tight-lipped too, and answered each question in an abrupt and biting few words. I tried repeating the questions and asking them in different ways, but to no effect. I'd guessed the director would want me to do something quickly, so in my dialogue I made reference to a VT (videotape) we had that was planned for later in the running order, but which I knew would be ready to cut to. The director picked up on my verbal cue for the VT and said in the earpiece, 'It's here,' so I introduced it and we cut from the studio floor for a few minutes to regroup. Whilst the VT played we brought in a second guest planned for later in the running order; when we came back to studio I introduced the new guest and was able to bounce the same questions off both of them. This worked much better, and with a colleague to 'share the load' the original guest relaxed and became very personable again.

Michael O'Donoghue, Higher Education producer/manager;
presenter, Distance Learning  TV

By this point you should be aware of what is required of a presenter and how to achieve it. Now, on to the business of how to enter the industry.

PART FOUR

# Getting a Job

## Where to train

**❝** I did presenting courses and workshops at various establishments before on-the-job experience. Becoming an accomplished presenter is about practice.

Howard Corlett, winner, *Sky Search for a Presenter*, 2006;
presenter, *The Seven Wonders of the Weald* (Sky)

Video-recording equipment and editing software has never been more accessible and affordable. Reality TV, citizen journalism, webcams, digital recorders of all kinds have made it possible for ordinary people to morph from media consumers to media producers, presenters and celebrities. There is a proliferation of video courses and media courses, as well as internet streaming websites – it has never been easier to record yourself and transmit your work. What need is there for training, you may ask? To a certain extent, the more you practise, the easier it gets, but what if you need more expert feedback or professional facilities? Good-quality training is part of the process to help get your career off to a good start, and it helps maintain industry standards.

A simple search on the internet will reveal hundreds of TV-presenting courses, ranging from one day to one week to one year, full-time, part-time, daytime, evening, in higher education, further education, adult education, drama schools, short courses, open classes, private one-to-one tuition, in studios, in rooms, with or without raw footage, with or without an edited showreel!

Many presenters find it useful to combine different kinds of training:

**❝** I did an intensive one-day course, a subsequent showreel, a two-day course at the Actors Centre, and a two day course at the City Lit.

Lesley Anne Webb, presenter,
Ravensbourne College in-house training courses

Some universities, such as Bedfordshire and Salford, include TV presenting within Media Performance courses; and Journalism courses like those at Goldsmiths or City University in London, or University College Falmouth, include TV reporting. UCAS will provide a useful starting point if you wish to study presenting, radio, journalism or broadcast journalism within a higher education setting. Higher-education courses can be funded by student loans or bursaries as they fall within the state system, but do think about the duration, commitment and the all-round academic study required – it's not just a vocational training.

It is rare to find TV-presenting tuition at theatre schools, but one of the top-ranking drama schools, the Academy of Live and Recorded Arts (ALRA) in London, includes TV presenting and a showreel in the final year of their BA (Hons) Acting degree. For part-time courses check your local adult-education centres – in London, for example, the City Lit has several to choose from.

Further-education courses and short courses can be found nationwide, offering a host of related skills such as public speaking, vocal tuition, relaxation techniques, scriptwriting, journalism, video skills, radio presenting, performance and presentation skills. Specific training centres for actors, such as the Actors Centre in London and Manchester, run specialised classes in presenting and performance techniques, plus very useful skills such as memorising scripts.

Short courses tend to fall within the private sector, so you will need to fund the training yourself. Most degree courses are selective, and some short courses will interview. Many private courses do not have any prerequisites: provided you can pay the fee, you are usually accepted on the course.

Radio presenting has close ties with TV presenting, and there are transferable skills from one to the other. Some universities, such as Sunderland, Lincoln and Bedfordshire, specialise in Radio, and the Broadcast Journalism Training Council (BJTC) lists accredited courses, such as those at the National Broadcasting School in Sussex. The BBC has free online training in radio, television, journalism and production techniques, which is a great resource. It does not replace face-to-face training, but it can be used in addition to that, and in your own time at home.

Dozens of courses and training options can also be found in publications such as *The Stage* and *Contacts*, the latter published by Spotlight. The option you choose may depend on your circumstances, location and budget, but it is also worth considering what you require from training.

Identify the skills gaps you want to work on, whether it be your on-screen performance, interviewing technique, scriptwriting skills, reading from a prompt, location walking and talking, multi-camera studio experience, vox pops or a particular genre. Feedback on your work is important and the best way to learn, so find out if the course you are considering involves viewing your recordings and assessing them; if you can evaluate your own work it will enable you to carry on improving after you have left the course. Enquire how many other people are on the same course, and how much on-screen time you will have. Although it can be useful to see how others approach the tasks, you may get frustrated if they take up your precious recording time. Most courses are taught by industry experts, but it is always worth checking who your tutors will be.

Some courses offer training and a showreel over a very short space of time, perhaps one or two days. I feel that these are best suited to people who have already taken some kind of tuition or preparation, otherwise the finished reel may just be a record of your training. Glossy showreels can be great fun to make and to own, but from experience I would suggest thorough training is needed first of all.

Certificates offered at the end of some short courses can sound attractive, but a certificate to say you have attended a presenting course will not get you a job. What producers want to see is how you present in an audition or screen test, so don't be over-reliant on an impressive-looking piece of paper.

Continuing professional development is undertaken by professionals in many fields as people continue learning and top up their skills throughout their careers. You may find you need to do more than one type of training to cover all the ground, establish your style, enter the industry, gain credits and consistently achieve a performance you are proud of. You should aim for a sensible mix of training, rehearsal and industry experience. One word of warning: non-selective private courses could attract people who in all likelihood will not make it as TV presenters, but no one has told them the truth. Don't become a 'course junkie' – but, on the other hand, don't run before you can walk!

Further information is available in the section on showreels and the Resources section in the Appendix.

**❝** I would definitely recommend a few individual lessons. I learnt so much in my lessons, and the focus was completely on me, so in an hour's session you can cover a lot. Practise in front of the camera and in front of the mirror at any point to allow yourself to build confidence in front of the camera.

Seema Pathan, presenter,
Price-drop TV, Bid TV, The Business Channel

❝ A lot of really good shopping-channel presenters have had a background in radio presenting. This is a good training ground as radio presenting is usually unscripted and the presenters often have to 'fill' or 'pad' and also talk to time.

Presenters who have not worked in television but have a background in sales often make good shopping-channel presenters. If you understand the principles and techniques to drive sales, you will find it easier to talk about any random product.

If you have a passion for shopping then your genuine enthusiasm will come across.

Public speaking or debating, commercial awareness and/or knowledge of sales would all be beneficial.

Del Brown, Live Director and Vision Mixer,
QVC, Express Shopping Channel, Challenge Jackpot

❝ The technical training of using in-ear talkback and multi-camera set-ups is invaluable, as is experiencing different presenting styles and formats like news, chat shows and shopping channels. Voice and movement tuition really helps with looking, feeling and sounding relaxed in front of the camera. Any kind of production or journalistic experience is also a plus point, as a lot of the time you will be writing your own links.

Nicci Brighten, presenter,
*Love Your Home Show*, 2008, Radio Wey 87.9 FM

Being in TV studios, in almost any role, is useful. You could apply to be a contestant in TV quiz shows, which will help you to feel familiar with being on set – and you might even win a prize! I know presenters who are stand-ins for celebrities: again, you will get to work on set and possibly read prompts. Or if you would rather observe, then apply to be in the studio audience during recordings, and you will see at close quarters how presenters go about their job. Audience tickets are freely available (see the Resources section in the Appendix).

Hopefully this will inspire you to feel that TV presenting could be within your reach, and that in the not-too-distant future you might have completed enough training to start looking for jobs. You will need a CV to accompany your job application. The next section gives some tips.

## Create a presenting CV

A CV (curriculum vitae) is essentially a current document of the skills you can offer a potential employer. What CV should you submit when applying for a TV-presenting job? How do you write a TV-presenting CV if you do not have much, or any, TV-presenting experience? What do you include and what should you leave out?

Start by reading through your current CV – what does it say about you? Does it give the impression that you are really an actor/lawyer/housewife, etc., who would like to be a TV presenter? Does your career history look like a patchwork of various jobs and experiences without a thread to pull them together?

Typically, an actor's CV starts with hair colour, eye colour, height, shoe size, weight, then lists theatre, film and TV acting credits chronologically. Physical details are not required for a presenting CV – if you submit a photo and/or showreel it will be quite clear what you look like. Your vital statistics are mostly used by wardrobe departments, but as presenters usually provide their own clothes you need not include those details either.

Whatever career you have come from and however impressive your achievements, try to see your CV from the point of view of the person most likely to be reading it – the TV producer. TV producers are busy people; they may have to sift through several CVs from potential presenters each week, and when a job advert is published there could be hundred of CVs that need to be looked at. Will they have time to interpret every line of your employment record to try and work out if you could present their new TV series? If you have a proven track record in presenting, then your credits should speak for themselves. If your presenting credits are on the thin side, or you are just starting out, how can you prove to the producer that you can cope with the demands of a live studio programme or fast-turnaround location recording?

The answer is to create a skills-based CV. This format will enable you to extract the appropriate skills from your previous jobs, experiences, placements and qualifications to make your employment history look as if it has all been aiming for this job. Think about the skills and qualities which a good TV presenter should possess, and which the TV producer may be looking for: the ability to think on your feet, create ad-lib or scripted material, bring out the best from an interviewee, research and write pieces to camera, perform in public, speak to camera, understand a brief, convey key points to the viewer and work in a live-broadcast environment.

Trawl through your current CV and past experiences and identify what skills you possess that are relevant and transferable. Have you ever recorded to camera, delivered live presentations, created publicity or PR material, been a live host, been interviewed in the media, worked in TV production, spoken in public, worked in retail or telephone sales, performed at children's parties, acted in or voiced corporate videos, performed onstage, written for newspapers or magazines in print or online, asked questions of members of the public, worked with presenters on TV or radio, presented any radio, worked on community television, taught or worked as a teacher or lecturer?

At the top of the CV put your name, and immediately alongside it, the words 'TV presenter'. Start to think like a presenter – you must be a presenter from the time you apply for the job. The person reading your CV needs to feel that you *are* a presenter, not a wannabe or just 'having a go'.

Create an opening statement to help define who you are. You should mentally be preparing for the interview. When asked 'Why should we employ you?', 'What kind of presenter are you?' or 'What have you got to offer?', you should have honed it, thought of the answers, and be able to sell your skills. Find the succinct phrases that describe you and include them at the top of the CV.

Add in your passions, interests, qualifications and education. Include the presenting genres that most interest you, and convince the employer that you are motivated. Devise appropriate headings to provide evidence of your skills.

What if you see more than one job advert that attracts you? I would suggest that you have more than one CV, tailored to the specific vacancies; in the same way you should have bespoke covering letters, and even different headshots and reels that are fit for the relevant purpose. Daytime and travel programmes are quite closely linked, but children's and shopping could require different approaches. You can try for a few areas until one takes off. Again, think like a producer. Would you rather choose from a specialised showreel or one which has a bit of everything in it, implying the presenter cannot make up his or her mind about which area to aim for?

There are many internet sites and books offering CV advice, different formats and layouts, and self-analysis tools to help discover your personality, strengths and weaknesses. Your first CV will not be your last! It is an organic document that should develop and improve as your credits and experience change. Look at presenting job sites and see what CVs others have submitted and which format might work for you.

Here are a few examples of CVs people have sent me in the past – before we worked on them, and after. Make it easy for the reader to see at a glance what transferable and relevant skills you have. For reasons of confidentiality I have deleted or changed some personal details.

*CV sample 1 (pages 134–5)*

The revised CV is skills-based, rather than chronological. It includes a personal statement, presenter skills, a presenting credit, and highlights compère work, corporate presenting jobs, journalism and PR skills.

*CV sample 2 (pages 136–7)*

The updated CV includes a presenting credit, a statement geared towards presenting and presenter-training skills. It highlights presenting and TV-production experiences such as compèring, vox pops and a TV-researcher role. It also includes a further TV-presenter training course.

*CV sample 3 (pages 138–9)*

The new CV includes punchier description and statements, and highlights TV-presenting skills and TV-presenter training.

*CV sample 4 (pages 140–41)*

The new-look CV has no extra presenting credits, but now looks like a presenting CV. It starts with the title 'Presenter', there is a statement to encapsulate what this presenter has to offer, the TV-presenting credits are emphasised with clear descriptions of the skills employed, and the production companies and broadcasters have been added. Relevant live presenting, journalistic experience and skills are included.

*CV sample 5 (pages 142–3)*

I was sent the final CV by one of my presenters, who after some training was successful at her first two presenting auditions. I thought the CV was clearly laid out, and it emphasised skills relevant to presenting. I didn't change anything on this one!

## CV sample 1 – before

```
                      Name: Jo Prince
         Address: 99 Carnival Road, East Hillstead.
                      Email: 99@home.com
                      Nationality: Irish
                         DOB: 20.05.80
```

**Relevant Experience:**

| | |
|---|---|
| Harries Foundation | Learning Mentor |
| | Supporting students who have been excluded from mainstream education |
| Greenfarm Theatre Company | Education consultant/ workshop leader |
| | Advising on and facilitating workshops at primary/secondary level |
| Exit Theatre Company | PPA cover teacher |
| | Providing curriculum-based drama lessons on a supply basis |
| Canning Post 16 Unit | SEN teaching assistant |
| | Supporting students with a variety of learning and/or physical difficulties |
| Whitefield Theatre Company | Artistic Director |
| | Managing my own private drama tuition service |
| Canvas Productions | Location research, |
| | compiling information for shooting scripts |
| Data Communications | PR Executive on campaigns |
| | Press liaison: researching/writing press releases, creative input |
| Atlas Magazine | Reporter |
| | Theatre/TV reviewer |
| Northwick Evening Telegraph | Junior Columnist |
| | Theatre/TV reviewer |

**Education:**
University of Dublin   Film & Literature BA Hons
Aries School of Acting PG diploma

**Skills:**
Scriptwriting, good Spanish, Russian and Italian, IT skills, Makaton sign language, full clean driving licence

**Interests:**
Film, theatre, fashion, art, food, netball

Over the past ten years I have also worked as an actor, including TV drama, therefore I am familiar with the demands of working on set and on location.

## CV sample 1 – after

> Name: Jo Prince – TV Presenter
> Address: 99 Carnival Road, East Hillstead.
> Email: 99@home.com
> Nationality: Irish
> DOB: 20.05.80
>
> I have a proven track record in journalism and PR; I am good in front of a camera; I work exceedingly well with people from all backgrounds; I always produce work of a highly professional standard.
>
> PRESENTING EXPERIENCE:
> August 2007      Garden City College College, in-house presenter
> *Live presenting using multi-camera, interview, ad lib and vox pop.*
>
> Mar–Sep 2006      Brown's Summer Resorts, Main Stage Compère
> *Live links between acts, hosting quizzes, competitions, bingo calling, the works!*
>
> Jun 2005      Withern Council, Presenter corporate video
> *Scripted to camera presenting*
>
> April 2002      FA Premier League Hall of Fame Compère
> *Liaising with assembled press, interviewing guests for promotional videos*
>
> JOURNALISM/PR EXPERIENCE:
> Canvas Productions, Researcher
> *Location research, compiling information for shooting scripts*
>
> Data Communications, PR Executive (campaigns include Stella Screen, Dunlop Slazenger)
> *Press liaison; Researching/writing Press Releases; Creative input*
>
> Atlas Magazine, Reporter
> *Theatre/Television Reviewer*
>
> Northwick Evening Telegraph, Junior Columnist
> *Theatre/Television Reviewer*
>
> TELEVISION EXPERIENCE:
> ITV drama, *The Pride*, Nancy (lead role); director Jake Adams
> BBC drama, *The Long and the Short*, Catherine (lead role); director Ged Harris
>
> TRAINING:
> University of Dublin – Film and Literature BA Hons
> Aries School of Acting – PG Diploma; Acting
>
> SKILLS:
> Scriptwriting, good Spanish, Russian and Italian, IT skills, Makaton sign language, full clean driving licence
>
> INTERESTS:
> Film, theatre, fashion, art, food, netball

## CV sample 2 – before

**PERSONAL PROFILE**
I have an interest in people and high personal standards of quality and professionalism. I have spent a lot of time on film sets and enjoy working in the environment. I have a good understanding of how the industry works.

**KEY SKILLS**
Creativity, this was developed both during my time at Primetime and JRL Events. I welcome opportunities to develop and present new ideas
I work well in a team and have a lot of experience managing and working with different groups of people. I also thrive when working alone on my own initiative
Researching, organising and developing an assignment to meet the criteria of a brief, often under limited time pressures

**EXPERIENCE**
**Events Manager, Primetime (Apr 05-Jun 06):**
Solely responsible for devising, coordinating and organis-ing large bespoke events. Liaised with external suppliers including production teams and caterers. Organised pre-event site visits to determine suitability of a venue.

**Licensed Brand Executive, On the Case Ltd (Dec 04-Apr 05):**
Developed a new role within the Head Office. Responsible for planning a nationwide auditing campaign. Created and developed a Guide and bespoke support materials. Developed strong relationships with representatives at venues.

**Events Manager, JRL Events (June-Sept 06):**
Organising a team of 30 to promote the launch of a new product. Driving a team across the UK to different venues

**COMMERCIALS/TELEVISION**
*September 2000-January 2005*
*Alien Autopsy* with Ant and Dec
*Blockbuster* Corporate Training Video
*Lenor* Advertising Campaign
*I'm the Right Answer* (Dale Winton) LWT

**THEATRE WORK (DANCER)**
*September 2000-January 2005*
*Spirit of the Dance*          Touring to 15 countries
*Broadway and Hollywood*      Global Cruise Lines

**TRAINING AND QUALIFICATIONS**
Diploma in Musical Theatre: Childgrove Ballet School
Dance:                      Post-Advanced Standard in all
                            disciplines
A Levels:                   10 subjects A-C grades
Various Courses ncluding:   'Understanding the Camera'

Equity Member.

Full clean driving licence.

## CV sample 2 – after

I am twenty-six and have always been very interested in presenting. I have toured and danced abroad for a number of years and this has given me a good understanding of the theatre environment. Various acting and modelling jobs have given me experience in front of the camera and my work for Knee-High Productions as a researcher has given me a strong insight into TV production. I have gained as much experience as possible including working with Autocue, live talkback from the gallery and multi-camera work. I am energetic and proactive. Previous experience has equipped me well to deal with different time pressures, adapt to new environments and think on my feet!

PRESENTING EXPERIENCE
June 2006, Wessex College
> Presented live link show which included multi-camera studio work, interviews and vox pops, with talkback and Autocue.

April 2005-June 2006, FAB company
> Hosting/compèring live presentations

March 2006, Trader Ltd
> Corporate video presentation

February 2002-2004, Global Cruise Lines
> Producing and presenting items for onboard TV channel including interviews, vox pops and live events on a weekly basis

TELEVISION – RESEARCHER
September 2006–Present, Knee-High Productions
> Sourcing contributors
> Contents package and location research
> Compile information for shooting scripts
> Providing support on filming days

COMMERCIAL/TELEVISION INCLUDES:
*Alien Autopsy* with Ant and Dec (feature film)
*I'm the Right Answer* with Dale Winton (LWT)
*Lenor* advertising campaign

THEATRE WORK INCLUDES:
*Spirit of the Dance*
*Spirit of Broadway*
*Broadway and Hollywood*

TEACHING EXPERIENCE
| | |
|---|---|
| Street-dance Class | Looking Good Health Club |
| Keep-fit Teacher | Global Cruise Lines |

TRAINING AND QUALIFICATIONS
| | |
|---|---|
| Diploma in Musical Theatre: | Childgrove Ballet School |
| Various Courses Including: | 'Children's TV Presenting' |
| | 'Understanding the Camera' |

## CV sample 3 – before

---

Name, address and e-mail supplied

PROFILE
I have an open and friendly nature. I have
five years' beauty-sales experience at award-
winning Gordon's Spa and have received
accreditation for outstanding sales. I have
the propensity to always succeed my targets.
I am a highly driven individual with diverse
skills who thrives on challenge.

QUALIFICATIONS
NVQ Level II and III Beauty and Holistic
Therapies
Reiki Master/Teacher Degree Sept 2007
Professional Membership of the Association of
Therapy Lecturers
TV Presenting for Beginners
Certificate of Merit at the Hilman Course for
Presenting

EXPERIENCE
June 1999     Black hair and Beauty Magazine
                Hair Model
Nov 2007      Appearance on BBC Two Roads
                Radio
Apr 2009      Radio interview on *The 4pm Show*
                to promote the benefits of
                massage therapy
(*Follow this link to listen to the interviews*)
Feb 2010      Article published on hair and
                beauty in *Friends* magazine
(*Follow this link to read the article*)
Web-presenter for local community TV in
Herronshire

References supplied

---

*CV sample 3 – after*

NAME, ADDRESS AND E-MAIL SUPPLIED
## TV PRESENTER

MOTIVATION

I am a natural communicator and I love the challenges of presenting. I am highly driven, energetic and have a positive attitude. I am able to work professionally and in a live broadcasting environment and also take direction. I work well under pressure, improvising and writing pieces to camera and have the propensity to always succeed my targets.

SKILLS

Guest/Expert on live broadcast for BBC Two Roads Radio (Nov 2007–Present)
*The 4pm Show* to promote the benefits of beauty and holistic therapies
Follow this link to listen to the interviews

Regular 'as live' reporting spots on Herronshire community TV (Oct 2008–Present)
Follow this link to listen to the interviews

- Researching and writing pieces to camera
- Working with Autocue
- Devising and creating idea
- Creating, writing and publishing articles
- Freelance writing for hairandbeautyjobs.com detailing my experiences within the beauty industry.

QUALIFICATIONS

- NVQ Level II and III Beauty and Holistic Therapies
- Reiki Master/Teacher Degree Sept 2007
- Professional Membership of the Association of Therapy Lecturers

TRAINING

- General Presenting Course
- Certificate of Merit at the Hilman Presenting Course, Apr 2007
- Showreel TV Presenting Course, Sept 2008
- One-to-one professional TV-presenter training, Jan 2009

HOBBIES AND INTERESTS

I love travelling and meeting interesting new people from different cultures and backgrounds. I enjoy salsa dancing, operatic singing, skiing, running, charity work, reading and going to the theatre.

References supplied

## CV sample 4 – before

```
Name:       Frankie Lowland  Height:       5'7"
Address:    3A Hill Close     Dress Size:   14
            Parton New Town   Hair:         Brown
            Kent              Eyes:         Brown
Tel:        01111 555444
email:      fl@123.net

EXPERIENCE
TV Presenting
     Presenter on pilot TV show
     Presenter for weekly show about music
     scene.
     Presenter at local community channel
     (Lighthearted documentary)
     (Host of studio discussion)
     (Sole presenter of series, 12 episodes to date)

TV Advertisements
Air Fresh       (Speaking part) May 2008
Golden Drops    (Speaking part) May 2008
BT              October 2007
Breakfast Bars  July 2006
Garden Sheds    (Featured extra) May 2004

Corporate
Ray, Smith      May 2008
and Dune

Films
The Hill        (Extra) October 2008
You, Me and It  (Extra) July 2007
Say When        (Extra) Feb 2008

TV
Cook In         (Featured extra) February 2009
Try Your Hand   (Contestant) December 2008
Weblinx         (Journalist, speaking part)
                September 2008
Crime Story     (Reconstruction) May 2008
Hair and        (Contestant) October 2007
Beauty Live     & April 2008
Have a Go!      (Contestant. 3 shows)
Summer Life     (Extra) April 2007
Rainbows        (Extra) October 2007

Voiceover
Car alarms      (Radio and TV ad) June 2008
Cholesterol     (Radio ad) December 2006
check
Dance studio    (Voiceover) December 2006
Marybelle       (Character voice, musical) May 2006
Showreel at www.youtube.com
```

## CV sample 4 – after

---

PRESENTER

Name:Frankie Lowland    Address:3A Hill Close, Parton New Town, Kent
Tel:    01111 555444    E-mail:  fl@123.net

A lively presenter with a passion for communication, I thrive on interacting and enabling people to tell their story on camera.

EXPERIENCE

TV PRESENTING

*What's Your Story?* (pilot)    Green Productions    Jan 09
- Presented to camera
- Researched and conducted interviews with experts
- Generated ideas for locations, interviews and topics to include in pilot

*Local Life* (series)    New World TV    May 08–
- Presented 12 episode series, 2 studio interviews and stand-alone documentary involving pieces to camera, interviews and managing audience discussion
- Generated ideas for shows
- Wrote scripts and questions
- Liaised with guests and contacts at venues to prepare them for interviews and discussions
- Currently working on second series of *Local Life*

*Music Scene*    Bottle Top Productions    Jan–Sept 08
- Researched, scripted and conducted interviews with musicians for show on multimedia platform including screens in entertainment venues and website

LIVE PRESENTING

Pub quiz host    Top Beer Pubs    Dec 06–
- Writing questions, hosting quiz including asking questions, scoring teams and awarding prizes

Marketing Officer    Bush Road College    Jan 04–Oct 08
- Scripted and delivered presentations about college to over sixty schools and twenty businesses per year

OTHER RELEVANT EXPERIENCE

I have a background of working in, and teaching, Marketing and Event Management, which demonstrates that I am:
- Confident when meeting a range of new people
- A good team player
- Flexible and adaptable to change
- Calm under pressure

While presenting is my main passion I also have experience in a range of other related activities including:
- Acting in advertisements, TV shows, corporate productions and films including:
  Katie Smith    Pink Productions    Sept 08
  Journalist (speaking role in BBC drama, *Weblinx*)
- Modelling in print ads
- Voiceovers for a musical, radio and TV ads
- Appearing as a contestant in gameshows

Referees supplied

Showreel available at www.youtube.com

---

*CV sample 5*

## Mission Statement

My name is Jane and I am professional presenter and actress. I believe I have all the skills to be an asset to any potential employer. Vivacious, bubbly, sparkly and smiley. I am a highly motivated and hardworking graduate who has worked constantly in theatre and television for the past ten years. I have a kaleidoscope of skills in music, children's entertainment, magic, face painting, theatre and television – and am a mother to 3. I learn fast, think on my feet – am energetic, articulate and warm. Reliable, unique, determined and driven with a passion to succeed and shimmy all the way to the top!

## Presenting Credits

| | |
|---|---|
| **1940s Archive News Presenter** | **History Plus TV** |
| **Live Stunt Show Presenter** | **Rowe Theme Park** |
| **Live Puppet Show Presenter** | **Rowe Theme Park** |
| **Corporate Presenter** | **MJ Productions** |

Production won a Gold World Medal in the New York 2009 Film & Video Awards

**Live Children's Presenter**          **Various Events**

Presenting songs, ideas, games and crafts to children from 1-7. High-profile clients, live singing, instruments, compèring.

**Vocalist Presenter**          **X Artists**

Global performances involving singing performance and compèring. Presenting a set to various clients. Requires ad lib, thinking on feet, addressing large corporate or private functions.

## Presenting Skills

- Talking to camera, talking to time, scriptwriting
- Autocue, vox pops, demos and makes
- Interviews, working under pressure, ad lib
- Storytelling, highly motivated self-starter, reliable, team player
- Patience, happy nature, sight-reading, energetic, keen
- Sales at Harrods and Selfridges, London.

## Further Skills

- Professional actress with 10 years experience, live theatre, television, film (short and feature), touring, commercials.
- Professional singer (classical/jazz/musical theatre versatile mezzo soprano)

- Clarinet/saxophone/piano – read music.
- Professional Children's Entertainer and face painter. Twizzle Parties. Balloon modelling, arts and crafts.
- Mother of 3 – twins and another!
- Good ear for accents, driving licence.

## Employment

I have worked successfully in theatre, film and television for the past 10 years. Travelling around the world from The National Theatre, Malta to Madrid, Greece to Japan, Germany to Prague. I have sung and strutted, played and piped my way through television and commercials, short films and musicals in all sorts of bizarre and wonderful places giving me a solid grounding in presenting myself to other people and presenting for other people. Employers include X Artists, The Actors Church West End, Taurus Musical Developments, ABC Theatre Wales, Telemedia Israel, BBC, Discovery Home & Health, ITN, Channel 4.

## Training

**Kathryn Wolfe Presenting**                    **2009**

**ALRA**                                        **2001–2002**
**(The Academy of Live & Recorded Arts)**
Post-graduate Diploma in Professional Acting – performance, advanced singing, jazz dance, radio and television

**University of Clowes**                         **1998-2001**
BA Hons Degree 2:1 – scriptwriting, devising, performance, sound and lighting, radio, mask, directing, theatre history, theatre genre.

## Interests

Learning new skills, music, theatre, children's education, entertainment and development, adventure, new journeys, travel, spirituality, puppetry, mask, family, eating out, film, nutrition and healthy living, writing, poetry.

*'Life is full of beauty, notice it. Notice the bumble bee, the small child, the smiling faces. Smell the rain, and feel the wind. Live your life to the fullest potential and fight for your dreams'* (Howard Thurman)

## Creating a showreel

A showreel or showtape should showcase your talents – it should be long enough for the viewer to judge your abilities, and short enough to leave them wanting more. Between two-and-a-half to four minutes is enough. Think of the judging panels on high-profile TV talent contests like *Britain's Got Talent*, who assess potential in less than one minute. Your reel may be viewed by busy producers who may only give you a minute of their time. If they are interested in seeing more they may watch to the end – but don't rely on it!

So, why do you need a reel? Producers use showreels to help sort applicants into those worth considering and those who are not suitable. But they do not tell the whole story, as the recordings could be heavily edited. So, even if you have a great reel you may not automatically be given the job – expect to have at least an interview, and usually a screen test too. Think of your reel as a calling card; it should open doors, lead to introductions and hopefully gain you a job. It is not essential to have a reel for some starter jobs, and it is certainly not the case that the more you pay the better the reel will be.

Where do you start? Who will make the reel, where will it take place, and how much will it cost? There are dozens of companies who specialise in showreel production, ranging from those who provide training with showreels to those who will create your reel from supplied footage. Costs vary depending on whether the reel is part of a course or made by a sole editor creating your reel in a few hours. You can find lists of showreel services and editors via the internet, or in trade publications.

Bear in mind that at the beginning of your career, employers are looking for potential, and many new presenters have gained auditions using home-made reels. Do you own or can you borrow a camera? Could you buy a used or inexpensive one? Can you handle simple editing software or do you know someone who can? It is perfectly possible to shoot material in and around your home that will get you through the first hurdles of securing a job. Do not feel you need to set it in a glamorous foreign location, as your personality and skills will shine even if you shoot in your lounge or back garden.

What are the advantages and disadvantages of going to a professional service or going it alone? One benefit of doing it yourself is that the reel will be unique to you. If you participate in a showreel course, for reasons of efficiency it is inevitable that your reel will look very similar to all the others. A home-made reel might sacrifice technical quality, but it can still get you to the audition stage if your presenting style is good. If you make your reel on a course, consider how many people will also be shooting that day. If you make it yourself over time, you can have access to the equipment for longer, and build in plenty of rehearsals. On the other hand, a professional showreel will be directed and edited by industry experts who can give you feedback on your performance, whereas you may have to judge the DIY version yourself.

What content should you put on your reel? What kinds of scripts? Should you mix genres, such as children's with travel, or shopping with sport? I suggest that you have a showreel for each very different genre – do not diversify, as this could indicate that you aren't aware of the differences, and you may not be taken seriously. For example, you could mix travel with shopping as they are both a type of 'selling', but if you combine children's with current affairs you will be sending out confusing messages about what kind of presenter you are. If you are not yet sure which area to go for, create more than one kind of reel. In fact, the very act of creating a reel for a specific genre may help you to make up your mind if that is the area that really excites you.

A typical daytime-presenter showreel might include an interview, vox pops and a piece to camera, and work with a prompt if you have access to the equipment. A children's showreel could include a make, a story to camera, an action song, or a magazine item such as an activity or adventure. It could also feature an interview or piece to camera. A sports presenter's reel could feature a piece to camera at a live event, reading from a prompt, or an interview with a sporting personality. For a shopping-channel reel you should record a two- or three-minute demo of you selling a product. As shopping channels rarely use prompts it is not important to include that on this reel. On any of the above reels you could include a piece to camera introducing yourself, describing why you want to be a presenter – think about what best sells you.

You could consider the following checklist and adapt it to suit your own interests and style. Choose the options that feel right for you – it is a guide rather than hard and fast rules.

What to put on your showreel:

| | DAYTIME PRESENTER | CHILDREN'S PRESENTER | SPORTS PRESENTER | SHOPPING PRESENTER |
|---|---|---|---|---|
| Introduce yourself | ✓ | ✓ | ✓ | ✓ |
| Interview | ✓ | ✓ | ✓ | |
| Vox pops | ✓ | | | |
| Piece to camera | ✓ | ✓ | ✓ | |
| Reading from a prompt | ✓ | | ✓ | |
| Demo | | | | ✓ |
| Make | | ✓ | | |
| Telling a story | | ✓ | | |
| A song | | ✓ | | |
| Activity | | ✓ | | |

Remember not to make your reel longer than four minutes – and you should probably include fewer items than you would imagine. If each item is about one minute, then four items in total is about right. Val Horton, casting agent at New Faces, feels that one piece to camera and one interview is sufficient – the piece to camera would show how you relate to the viewer, and the interview would show how you relate to someone else on-screen. Val says:

    **" If possible we like to see a ten- to fifteen-second montage or split screen at the beginning of the reel (no longer) showing different looks or stills. This should be followed by a piece to camera and then an interview on a subject – preferably about which the presenter knows.**

What else should you bear in mind when shooting the items? I suggest that you include long takes such as walking and talking to camera – to prove you can! A producer would like to know that you can memorise and deliver a forty-five-second piece to camera. Even if this is not the first take, it does show some skill. If a showreel is heavily edited it can become a showcase for the editor rather than the presenter, and the producer may think you can only deliver ten seconds of material at a time.

Technical quality should be good, but it does not have to be broadcast quality. Though I once saw an advert for presenters which said that a piece to camera submitted on a mobile phone is acceptable.

You could check the criteria that producers and agents look for. Some agencies and channels give showreel advice on their websites. You can also contact agents direct and ask what they would like to see on a reel.

    **" We do not like to see the 'tailored' reels, as they usually come across as unnatural. If it is a first presenting reel we feel it is better to go out with a friend and put something together on digicam, since we can tell immediately if there is any talent.**

                    Val Horton, casting agent, New Faces

The Channel Five children's-programming website states that if you want to be considered to present *Milkshake*, you need to send a one- to two-minute (maximum) reel which should include you talking straight to camera and it does not have to be broadcast quality.

Your showreel should not be set in stone; like your CV, it is an organic artefact, which will evolve and develop. You should replace and add fresh material as you improve and gain credits. Adapt it for each job, use it for marketing purposes, and re-edit it according to feedback you receive.

Showreel checklist:

1. Check the website of the organisation/agent/channel you are applying for to see if they have specific criteria for your showreel.
2. Research, write and create your script material.
3. Working with a trusted friend or crew shoot and edit the pieces, assessing the best takes. Do retakes if necessary.
4. Load showreel footage on websites; e-mail showreel links to your contact list of employers; apply for auditions combining reel, CV, photos and covering letters, as appropriate.
5. Monitor feedback and adjust the reel as necessary.

Here is some showreel information from presenters:

**66** I did my first showreel on a course. My current one is edit three and only uses one piece from my original reel. The rest is from the cooking show I do on the Community Channel. I start with a piece to camera which relates to some vox pops, interspersed with other short pieces of me interviewing people and talking to camera within the items. I end with the closing piece to camera for the vox pops.

Cate Conway, presenter, *The Seven Thirty Show* (UTV), *Cooking in the Community* (Northern Visions)

❝ I used some footage that we had filmed on a course, then filmed some more pieces myself with a friend, and had someone else edit it all together. I have quite a few pieces to camera on entertainment, lifestyle and property subjects, both in the studio and outside. I also have a walking/talking piece and an interview done in the studio.

Charlie Lemmer, presenter,
Real Estate Channel, Dubai Eye, Abu Dhabi TV, Current TV

❝ I used *The Seven Wonders of the Weald* series, *Search for a Presenter* competition, Thomson TV and a little clip of me in the BBC's *Strictly Dance Fever* competition at the end.

Howard Corlett, winner, *Sky Search for a Presenter*, 2006;
presenter, *The Seven Wonders of the Weald* (Sky)

❝ My reel is all made of previous work, a mix of small clips and montage. A friend who has his own production company edited it for me.

Louise Houghton, presenter, sit-up channels and *SuperCasino*

❝ The one thing I would thoroughly recommend is buying a video camera. This way you can practise in front of the camera and film to build up your showreel.

Naomi Evans, presenter,
Ravensbourne College in-house training courses

## Where to find presenting jobs

❝ Remember the Four Ps – breaking into TV presenting takes Patience, Perseverance and Practise, Practise and more Practise! Always be well Prepared, so when that golden opportunity comes along you are ready to shine. And don't forget to believe in yourself!

Nicci Brighten, presenter,
*Love Your Home Show*, 2008, Radio Wey 87.9 FM

The presenting industry is overcrowded with people who 'want to be presenters', but to get to the head of the queue think about what you have to offer. List your interests, hobbies, qualifications – look at the range of niche channels and see where you might fit in. As I have already mentioned, people who attend presenting courses come from a wide variety of backgrounds. Think about what experiences and interests you can use to get a foothold in the industry. Your knowledge of vintage wine? Your yoga qualification? Your synchronised swimming? I know presenters who have used exactly these qualifications and interests to start their career.

### Internet Job Sites

One of the best ways to find presenting jobs is to trawl the websites that regularly list genuine job adverts, and go for auditions. Some sites are free, some are subscription, and you should aim for those offering the kinds of jobs that you can connect with. Many actors will already be familiar with this process – there are sites which combine acting and presenting jobs or specialise in presenting; some feature voice-over and radio-presenting jobs as well.

The jobs advertised on these sites can include high-profile ones, some of which have job descriptions that are deliberately vague, so that you may need to read between the lines. For example, if a programme such as *Blue Peter* advertised for a new presenter they would receive sacks full of applications, yet I have seen online adverts for shows such as this written along the lines of: 'Presenter wanted for popular children's programme.' In the same way, some highly popular shopping channels do not reveal their identity at first, so it is worth being astute. Some adverts sound very low-key indeed, such as broadcasting on the web or from home using a webcam; sometimes the pay might be low, but these jobs are still worth doing even if just for the experience.

*Internet presenting*

There are hundreds of internet TV channels such as mainstream and global Bloomberg TV; Belfast local-community TV Northern Visions; and specialised channels such as jewellery channel Gemondo TV. Web-presenting is also on the increase, where real presenters seem to pop out of the screen to introduce products and services. Although the viewing figures for some of these channels and sites are in the hundreds or thousands rather than millions, it could work in your favour. Even if the job is not in a field you are aiming for, it will give you confidence and experience, and add to your 'flying hours'. When the advert of your dreams comes along you will be in a better position to succeed at the audition. You can include all professional engagements in your CV as credits, and try to obtain a copy of the work for marketing purposes. And, if the job doesn't go according to plan, you will be grateful that it was *not* on mainstream TV!

Nigel Dacre is currently Chief Executive of Inclusive Digital TV, a digital media company he set up in 2007 that has created Kent.tv, Home2Home.tv and The Co-operative.tv:

❝ I think that the internet will undoubtedly increase the range of work available to presenters, as more organisations and companies either launch their own web TV channel or increase the number of videos on existing websites. The downside, of course, is that the economics of the internet means that the rates of pay for this kind of work will be significantly lower than on traditional TV.

*Low/No pay*

There is an area of work known as low/no paid, where you will be given a copy of the programme in lieu of payment. These jobs could include presenting on the internet, or for university or college television and media courses, many of which deliver highly professional productions. In fact I know many experienced and busy presenters who have taken these opportunities to add to their showreels, as many educational institutions are capable of producing light entertainment, chat shows and magazine programmes in their often professional-standard TV studios. Occasionally, though, the promised tape may not appear – this is usually because of technical errors rather than deliberate deception. Volunteering or offering your services for free to hospital radio and community TV are also excellent starting points.

*Broadcasters' websites*

Job vacancies can be placed on the websites of broadcasters, such as BBC, ITV and independent production companies, and they are free to access. As well as presenting, work experience in TV production is valuable, but the BBC receives over 20,000 applications per year for work experience, so think hard about why you want to apply. ITV also offers work experience – 1,000 jobs per year to over-eighteens. TV production is a tried and tested route into TV presenting, and many have started that way. It gives you an inside knowledge of production processes and what is expected of presenters. You may be working alongside household names, and you might convince the producer you could present some links to camera or vox pops. On the other hand, I also know some presenters who enjoyed production so much they have stayed there, rather than pursuing their original idea of presenting.

*Publications, and their associated websites*

As well as the internet, jobs are advertised in newspapers and trade publications such as *The Guardian*, *The Stage*, *Broadcast* and *Televisual*. There are lists of production companies and their output in *Kemps*, *The Production Guide* and the *Producers Alliance for Cinema and Television (PACT) Directory*, all of which are available online and published as reference books.

## Personal contacts

The creative industries also operate by word of mouth, and if you know someone who knows someone who knows someone in TV, contact them and send them your reel. With research you can identify the production companies that make the programmes you are interested in, be that documentaries, travel or fashion. Find out who you can send your details to – it would usually be the production manager, producer or office manager.

## Cold calls

TV is your greatest resource! Although the end credits of many programmes are squeezed and flashed across the screen in seconds, you should note the names of producers or production companies and add them to your list. It does take time to 'network' and to create your own contacts book of producers and production companies, but this will be an invaluable source of people to approach now and in the future. Of course, this method of job hunting is hit and miss as you will not know if the companies are currently in production or if they are looking for a presenter, whereas if you answer a job advert at least you know there is a vacancy to be filled. However, for some successful presenters it has been a case of 'right time, right place', so it is always worth having a go.

*Competitions*

Presenter competitions can launch you from obscurity to fame, and are worth looking out for. Hermione Cockburn, science broadcaster known for BBC's *Fossil Detectives*, *Coast*, *What the Ancients Did for Us*, *Rough Science* and Teachers TV, won the BBC Talent 'Science on Screen' competition in 2002. There were 1,500 entrants and Hermione was voted the winner after two appearances on the *Tomorrow's World Roadshow* on BBC 1; she subsequently co-presented the *Tomorrow's World Awards* on BBC1. In 2007, Craig Rowe won QVC's 'Search for a Presenter' competition; Craig had previous presenting credits on travel channels. Newcomer Alan Mechem won GMTV's 'Sofa Factor' in 2008. Five thousand people applied and Alan, a teacher from Essex, had never tried presenting before. Even if you are not successful, taking part in competitions is invaluable experience, and may lead to something in the future.

*Self-promotion*

Finding jobs is not just about looking for vacancies, opportunities and competitions. It also requires self-publicity and marketing. Many of the internet sites that feature job adverts also offer a 'shop-window' service, where you can advertise your skills in categories such as sports, beauty, motoring or general. They will host your CV, photos and reel, and you can link from that site to your own website (if you have one). If you decide to sign up, keep your online CV up to date because the search criteria can be quite specific.

I know a producer who needed a male co-presenter to work on an existing technical-resource programme; she accessed a site which specialises in new presenters, typed in 'male, thirties, ICT literate' and discovered Matthew Tosh, a science teacher in Bristol. Matthew was given a screen test, then employed to present several series for Teachers TV, and he is now a successful, full-time broadcaster.

**❝** I'd long had an interest in television work. I was fascinated by the entire production process. I developed my own showreel with a friend who runs a small production company. At the same time, I signed up to StartinTV.com with an up-to-date CV. One Friday evening, I had a call from Jackie Andrews, a producer at Brook Lapping Education, who was searching for a presenter with experience of working with educational and IT resources. The following week, I was in the production office recording a screen test, and it wasn't long before I joined the rest of the production team on *Resource Review*.

Matthew Tosh, presenter, Teachers TV; guest presenter, *Ministry of Mayhem* (ITV), *Brainiac Live: Test Tube Baby* (Sky)

*Publicity material – photographs, showreel and CV*

You will need some headshots, a CV and a reel to promote yourself, but you do not have to spend a fortune on these. Have a look at other presenters on websites, in particular the successful ones, and see how they have marketed themselves. Your photos are important and should represent the real you. They should show expression and character, and you should think carefully about the image they portray. If you already have a flattering photo, you could try using that. Do not feel that you have to visit a professional photographer in the first instance, although if you can it might be a good investment. For further information about photographers see the Resources section in the Appendix.

Most job adverts ask for a sample of your work, either a showreel or a CV, or both. See previous sections on how to create these essential tools to market yourself to potential employers.

*Agents*

TV presenting is an open-access industry and does not rely on having an agent to make introductions and secure work for you – it is perfectly possible to find your own work. However, an agent will open more doors, have industry contacts at a high level, and an authority within the profession. An agent will also handle paperwork like contracts, invoices, membership of professional bodies, as well as marketing and career advice. There are hundreds of agents in the UK, but they receive dozens of requests for representation each week, so to interest an agent you will need to supply a showreel and evidence of professional commitment and potential. In return for their service, agents will take commission – usually ten or fifteen per cent. It is not necessary to have an agent at the start of your career, but as your career takes off you should try and get representation. There is a lot of useful advice in *Contacts* (and also see the section on agents for more information).

*Directory listing*

*Spotlight Presenters* is a publication which, like the long-established *Spotlight*, is a directory of talent. It features hundreds of professional presenters with their photo, main credits and contact details, and is used by TV and radio stations, production companies, advertising agencies and casting directors to source presenters. In order to be considered for entry in *Spotlight Presenters* you need to be over eighteen years and have some training in drama or presenting, possibly some expert knowledge, and you will need to have professional broadcast experience.

As the market is growing so quickly, there is a newer section called 'Emerging Talent' which is for those who have had some training but lack broadcast experience. Included in the price of membership, you are given half an hour of studio time at the Spotlight offices in Leicester Square,

London, to record pieces to camera; these can be loaded up on to the Spotlight website for potential employers to see. Membership will also entitle you to receive hundreds of job adverts per week via Spotlight Link.

If you use the internet for job-hunting and promotion, the money you save on DVD duplication and postage can be put towards training, photos and shooting material – but you will still need bags of confidence, tenacity and motivation. Try your hand at more than one area of presenting and see which takes off. Many presenters get established in a parallel genre such as print or radio – and when you have a track record in one area it is easier to transfer to another, or keep both jobs going for a portfolio career. Also consider being an interviewee or guest expert – there are internet sites that specialise in sourcing experts for broadcasting. If you have made a successful appearance as an interviewee, you could be given your own slot.

There are dozens of job-advert sites, some of which are listed in the Resources section in the Appendix. The more experience you have in this area, the better, as you will discover what is expected of you in an audition.

❝ I belong to Spotlight, Presenter Promotions and Production Base.

Denise Ching, guest presenter, QVC

❝ I scour the net looking for opportunities on mandy.com.

Cate Conway, presenter, *The Seven Thirty Show* (UTV),
*Cooking in the Community* (Northern Visions)

❝ I got a job as a runner at *Sky Sports News*, which is where I realised that I wanted to be a TV presenter. I then had some presenting lessons, after which I started to apply for auditions. A couple of months later I landed my first contract with Bid TV.

Seema Pathan, presenter,
Price-drop TV, Bid TV, The Business Channel

**"** My acting agent sent me to some presenting screen tests. Since then I have just tried to send out as many showreels as possible to production companies. I set up a database on my laptop with contact details for production companies and agents. I initially send out my showreel to each contact and then after a few months I send them a card with my details on it to try and jog their memory. I carry business cards with me which have all my details and a photo on, and try and give these out at every opportunity. Courses are good to meet new people and get new leads. Lastly, internet sites are useful and I have gained a few jobs through StarNow.

Charlie Lemmer, presenter,
Real Estate Channel, Dubai Eye, Abu Dhabi TV, Current TV

**"** I won *Search for a Presenter* on Sky with LifeTV and had a series broadcast as the prize.

Howard Corlett, winner, *Sky Search for a Presenter*, 2006;
presenter, *The Seven Wonders of the Weald* (Sky)

**"** Whist working at regional dance radio station Vibe FM, I took part in a documentary for *Anglia Tonight*. I was then asked to come in for an interview for the weather job at Anglia. (I got it!)

Becky Jago, presenter, *Anglia Tonight*, *Newsround*,
*Sky Sports News*, GMTV's *Entertainment Today*

**"** In 2006, I entered *Search for a Presenter* on Sky's LifeTV. Hundreds of people entered and I ended up in the final three. I didn't win but a few weeks later Life asked if I would be interested in working with them on a series called *Dress My Mate*. This built me for my chosen career ahead, I learnt loads, some good, and some bad! I definitely learnt I need an agent to deal with my fees! It was hard work, we had to film two half-hour shows in one day, and it was a six-part series, by day three I couldn't feel my feet! But it was a fab experience.

Jill Kenton, presenter, jnetradio.com, Hayes FM, QVC,
*Dress My Mate*; contributor, *BBC Breakfast*

**"** After realising I was being seen as a wannabe presenter rather than someone who could seriously do the job, I realised I needed to train properly and that for me it would take more than one or two days on a TV-presenting course. I spent a whole academic year learning broadcast journalism and radio from the ground up. After graduating I found the official qualification really served to open doors. I began newsreading and reporting on local BBC radio, and soon began to present my own weekend show. This led to a co-presenting position on national radio and then from there I started to present travel videos, make regular appearances on TV, as well as writing for high-profile internet sites and the national press. I am sure some people are lucky and they go from wannabe to fully fledged presenter in a short period of time, but for me that wasn't going to be enough.

Lisa Francesca Nand, presenter, talkSPORT radio, Sky Travel; guest presenter, *Sky News*; journalist

**"** I worked on the *European Drag Racing Championships* as a production assistant, and when the company dropped it I applied direct to the company who took the show over – and ended up getting my first presenting job there.

Louise Houghton, presenter, sit-up channels and *SuperCasino*

**"** I spoke at 'The Mind of an Entrepreneur' show at Kensington Olympia. MTV were at the show interviewing the speakers and presenters, so I did an interview with them after my workshop. A couple of years later the MTV interviewer was on the panel of a show that was looking for a presenter to do a regular thirty-minute slot and she remembered and recommended me to the show producer.

Marilyn Devonish, presenter, *The Life Success Show* (Sky)

**"** I broke into presenting by accident! A friend needed someone to present an introduction to a short movie they had made.

Luke Tudball, presenter,
Ravensbourne College in-house training courses

**66** I was doing a local radio roadshow and a local TV company said, 'Hey, we would love you to do presenting for us.' I immediately called over my colleague who unfortunately took over and said everything that I thought of! Lesson one – maybe being sharing and giving means that someone else will get in before you do!

Karin Ridgers, founder/presenter, veggievision.tv

**66** I was very fortunate to be invited to a college to be a presenter on their directing course. I did this every couple of months over about two years. It was brilliant to have regular practice at being in front of the camera, without the focus being mainly on you. This gave me great confidence, and helped me to find out which type of presenting I was most suited to, and which areas needed more honing. There is still so much to learn! I then applied for a presenting job on Talent Circle, and got the job!

Fiona Watkins, presenter,
Holmwood's English Listening Training

Once you have found the jobs and applied for them, you will need to prepare for auditions.

## What happens in presenting auditions

A TV-presenting audition can range from a chat in a room with a producer to a 'live' skills-based test in a multi-camera studio with in-ear talkback and a prompt – and anything in between!

Aim to go for as many auditions as you can, especially at the start of your career. Even if you are not successful at a particular audition, you will gain confidence, meet producers, and hopefully impress the employers so they will bear you in mind for next time, or possibly for another job in the pipeline.

Your showreel may have sparked some interest from a producer, but you will need to prove that you can actually present to camera without going wrong or fluffing. A programme may require you to perform specific tasks, such as using props, interviewing children, or selling in a particular style. The producers at the audition will want to assess how well you perform under pressure, and how well you take direction.

You may be going for an audition for a programme you have never heard of – that doesn't matter. There are hundreds of smaller channels and production companies producing output for digital TV or internet viewing. The job may be low or even no pay, but you could still benefit from the experience. If you have good audition technique, when the job or audition comes along that you really want, you will be better equipped for it.

Prepare by researching and practising audition tasks. For example, if you are told the audition will involve talking about a topic for two minutes, then rehearse it to time. If the programme or channel is on air, study what the style the current presenters use, and what they wear. Walk in looking like you could fit in and be the face of the channel. It goes without saying that you must get to the audition in plenty of time, relax and go through your notes and ideas.

I know a presenter who has just had a successful audition for a major shopping channel. She prepared her product and demo thoroughly, wore an appropriate dress and accessories, planned her presentation very well, and impressed the producers so much they commented on her professional attitude – it was as if she was about to go live on air. All her hard work paid off and she has been given a job on the channel.

Bear in mind that auditions can also resemble a cattle market! You will rarely be offered any rehearsal time. You will be given a time slot, so you must be ready to perform and confident. Auditions are usually recorded.

There are no set formats for auditions. Here is a fairly comprehensive guide to the kinds of tasks that can crop up – but be prepared for anything!

| | DAYTIME PRESENTER | CHILDREN'S PRESENTER | SPORTS PRESENTER | SHOPPING PRESENTER |
|---|---|---|---|---|
| Ad lib talk to camera about yourself | ✓ | ✓ | ✓ | ✓ |
| Be an interviewer/ interviewee | ✓ | ✓ | ✓ | ✓ |
| Speak to time | ✓ | ✓ | ✓ | ✓ |
| Memorise a script | ✓ | ✓ | ✓ | ✓ |
| Write a script | ✓ | | | |
| Reading from a prompt | ✓ | ✓ | ✓ | |
| Use in-ear talkback | ✓ | ✓ | ✓ | ✓ |
| Handling disasters | ✓ | | | |
| Demo | | | | ✓ |
| Make | | ✓ | | |
| Telling a story | | ✓ | | |
| A song | | ✓ | | |
| Activity | | ✓ | | |

Ad libbing about yourself could involve answering questions such as 'Tell us about yourself', 'Why do you want to be a presenter?' or 'Why do you want to present this programme?' You might be asked to memorise a script sent to you in advance, or given to you on the day. Coping with disasters could mean that the prompt 'accidentally' breaks down, or the timings on the interview might change – just to see how you cope. Auditions for children's programmes could involve any of the above tasks, but they can also include working with children, animals or both!

Shopping-channel screen tests can be fairly specific, usually asking you to demo a product to camera on your own for two or three minutes, or chat with the presenter about a product and demo it for ten minutes. You could be talking about a supplied product or one that you have selected yourself. You might be told what the tasks will be in advance, but be prepared to talk about any product they supply, which could be anything from a water bottle to a wooden peg! Most shopping channels do not use a prompt (although it is still possible that you might be asked to read from a prompt in the audition), but they do use talkback. Evidence of preparation is very important: if you are demonstrating a cooking utensil in an audition, bring the appropriate food to use during the demo, and prepare some typed notes on the points you want to cover with the presenter.

Some auditions pair you up with another candidate so you can take it in turns to be presenter one and presenter two. Some auditions set the presenter tasks in advance to rehearse, but on the day the producer might give an extra unprepared task. One jewellery channel asked a presenter to talk about eight different pieces of jewellery, in fine detail, with no preparation time before the day.

Sometimes auditions can take place over several rounds, gradually narrowing down the most successful candidates. The process could start with a recorded or unrecorded interview or chat with the producer, or an apparently simple task. In the case of children's programmes this could be reading a story aloud, or for shopping channels it could be to sell a product for one minute.

Do not be lulled into thinking that an informal approach will be any less rigorous than a more formal set-up. You will be judged from the moment you enter the building, and you may be asked questions about your background, motivation, skills or the programme genre.

The second round could be more realistic. It could be held in a studio, with more than one camera, a floor manager, a prompt, in-ear talkback. There could be more challenging tasks, such as working with longer scripts and sequences, possibly to time. Here are some real-life audition experiences from presenters.

66 One interesting experience was during the *Search for a Presenter* competition. The final consisted of being in a studio, having to fill to camera whilst hearing on my earpiece that the mystery guest would be late. When he finally arrived, along with his pet ferrets, I then had to interview him whilst trying to wrestle with the ferrets which were intent on hiding under my shirt! The only way to go was to just roll with it and have fun.

Howard Corlett, winner, *Sky Search for a Presenter*, 2006; presenter, *The Seven Wonders of the Weald* (Sky)

66 When I went for a screen test for a children's channel, I was e-mailed three tasks to prepare before the audition and I had a week to rehearse what I was going to do. In the studio there was just one camera, which I had to present to. In most auditions you are asked to prepare something in which you just talk to camera about yourself, so I would always think about what I was going to say; for example, why I want the job and why I want to be a presenter.

Naomi Evans, presenter, Ravensbourne College in-house training courses

66 Talking about a subject or an object for one, two or three minutes is a common audition task. This can range from the mundane to the downright obscure! Again, the best preparation for this is practising with general household or random objects. If you can talk at length about the wonders of a crab fishcake or an Andalusian prayer rug you might just have what it takes to go the distance.

Nicci Brighten, presenter, *Love Your Home Show*, 2008, Radio Wey 87.9 FM

❝ It's not possible to get every job that you might audition for. Prepare yourself to not actually get what you think might be your 'dream job', but have hope that the right thing will come along for you when the time is right. Try not to be what you *think* the people auditioning you will want you to be, just be yourself; it may be that you are just the type of person they are looking for! Try to remember the names of people that you meet at an audition – if you get a call back, they'll be really impressed that you've remembered their names! Keep a compact blotting powder on you, to check your teeth and give your face a light powder down before going in to audition too, so you're not embarrassed by any lunch in your teeth or having a shiny forehead (lighting guys will be grateful!).

Gemma Hunt, presenter, *Barney's Barrier Reef*,
*Xchange* (CBBC); guest co-presenter, *Smile*

## What happens in presenting interviews

An interview for a presenting job is similar to an interview for any other job. The main difference is that it could be combined with a screen test, and it could be recorded, or have recorded elements.

Carefully read the job description and specifications and see if your experience and interests fit the criteria. Find out about the channel, the company, the programme, watch the broadcasts, or seek out previous recordings on DVD, tape or the internet. Research any rival or competing programmes so you can talk about the field in general.

Think about, and practise, your answers to obvious interview questions such as:

- Why have you applied for this job?
- Why do you want to be a presenter?
- Why should we choose you for this job?
- What relevant experience do you have?

- What would others say are your strengths and weaknesses?
- Are you a team player?
- What do you do in your spare time?
- Explain your CV.

In addition, consider the not-so-obvious questions that could come up, such as:

- What makes you special as a presenter?
- What makes a good presenter?
- How do you connect with the audience?
- Who is the audience?'

The key personnel likely to be asking you questions are the producer and the director, but for high-profile jobs there could be a panel of people. Sometimes the interview is recorded to show to executives at a later date. Basic interview etiquette applies; look good, dress appropriately, be punctual, shake hands, be well-mannered, and, if requested, have one or two questions to ask of the panel to show you have given the job some thought. Maintain good eye contact with the panel, smile, eliminate nerves and turn off your mobile phone. Here are some thoughts from presenters who have had successful auditions and job interviews:

❝ I dress up smartly, get there in good time, then just play it by ear, being myself.

Charles Armstrong, corporate presenter, Inland Revenue, Marks & Spencer, Zurich, Online Casino Reports

❝ Learn about the role you are auditioning for and remember to take questions – research is key here. Interest in their business is always helpful along with a good audition.

Jill Kenton, presenter, jnetradio.com, Hayes FM, QVC, *Dress My Mate*; contributor, *BBC Breakfast*

**"** Research the producer, company or production. Look at their recent work, websites, etc. I like to be well informed.

Colette Redgrave, presenter, kent.tv

**"** It sounds obvious but you really have to make sure you know what you are talking about. If you are confident about your subject it makes the whole process a lot easier and will ensure you are relaxed and can focus on the job in hand. I have learned not to apply for anything I don't think I could at least feign some expert knowledge at. Keeping up to date with current affairs and popular culture means I have a wider area of knowledge and that fewer things stuff me up! I also make sure I know as much about the production company or broadcaster as possible. These days all it takes is a quick internet search to find out what programmes they make and who the people are you are going to be meeting. I then just try to relax and be myself.

Lisa Francesca Nand, presenter, talkSPORT radio, Sky Travel; guest presenter, *Sky News*; journalist

**"** As TV presenting is a visual medium, you have to look good in front of the camera. But it isn't just about face value. Ultimately, you need to be able to deliver. No matter how preened or polished you might look, you need to have done your preparation: research the company, find out what they specialise in, and take a look at previous output and the type or style of presenters they already work with.

Nicci Brighten, presenter,
*Love Your Home Show*, 2008, Radio Wey 87.9 FM

Hopefully you will make a good impression at your audition and interview. The following sections give some further tips on how, and who, to impress.

## Getting an agent

Getting an agent is much the same as getting a job: you will need to impress a potential employer with your showreel or audition and they will only take you on if they can use your talents; equally, an agent will only take you on if they like your reel and if they feel they can get you work.

Angharad Marsh, TV Talent Manager at Wise Buddah Talent, gives this advice to new presenters when looking for representation:

66 Have a passion. We meet so many presenters who feel that they could present 'anything' – it is refreshing and inspirational to agents when a potential client says they have an interest in something that isn't *T4* or MTV. A showreel is a must before any meeting. It is very rare that an agent will agree to a meeting without seeing their presenting skills first – asking a friend to film you at a concert, in your favourite shop or in your local park is a great start and only needs to be a maximum of three minutes.

How important is it to have an agent if you want to break into presenting? It is not essential, especially at the beginning of your career. It is much easier to enter the presenting industry without an agent than the acting profession, but if you want to get mainstream presenting jobs, having an agent will help. As already mentioned, an agent can open doors, advise on career management and handle the administration, contracts, invoices and paperwork associated with the jobs. Some production companies or broadcasters would rather go to an agent for recommendations than spend considerable amounts of time trawling through websites looking for a new face.

There are different kinds of agencies in the entertainment industry, from those who represent actors, presenters, voice-over artists, 'personalities', and after-dinner speakers, to those who are personal managers or who offer a diary service. You may find you need more than one agent to handle these different types of work: some agencies will happily handle presenting and voice-over bookings, while some acting agencies would rather concentrate on securing acting work but not presenting jobs. Your choice of agent can also depend on whether you tend to find most of your own work yourself, whether you need someone to find work for you, or simply organise your bookings.

Do your research to find out what kind of clients a particular agency has on their books, and which agency would be most likely to consider taking you on. Lists of presenter agents can be found in *Contacts*, which is a very useful source of general information about the scene. Some presenter agencies tend to have mostly newscasters, some specialise in presenters who work on entertainment programmes, and some are a mix of presenters and genres. You will impress an agency if you have found out what kinds of clients they represent.

Here are some well-known specialist agencies:

JAMES GRANT MEDIA   Represents top presenters mostly working in entertainment, such as Ant and Dec, Davina McCall, Ben Shephard, Holly Willoughby, Phillip Schofield, Piers Morgan, Richard and Judy, Simon Cowell, Vernon Kay and Reggie Yates.

ARLINGTON ENTERPRISES   Specialises in lifestyle and factual, representing presenters who work in categories such as wildlife, fashion, food and drink, gardening, motoring and property. Some top presenters on their books are Alan Titchmarsh, James May, Joe Swift, Alice Roberts, Rachel de Thame and Kirsty Allsopp.

BLACKBURN SACHS ASSOCIATES   Specialises in presenters who work on live events, and their talent list includes Clare Balding and Peter Alliss from BBC Sport, and the Gladiators.

KNIGHT AYTON MANAGEMENT  Specialises in news and current affairs, and their client list includes Fiona Armstrong, Jennie Bond, Jeremy Bowen, Michael Buerk, Jane Hill, Nicholas Owen, Jon Snow, Moira Stuart and Romilly Weeks.

There are agencies that have a mix of established and emerging talent, such as New Faces, managed by Val Horton and Tania Patti. Val Horton has been in the film and TV business for forty-five years – the last nine years as a casting agent at New Faces – and represents Amani Zain, Jill Kenton, and presenters on several shopping channels.

What skills and qualities does Val feel a presenter should possess?

❝ They should be instantly appealing, sparkly, bubbly and confident. In addition they should look interesting and good on-screen and be able to relate to an audience in a warm and friendly manner.

What does Val personally look for in a presenter?

❝ Talent! We look for someone with the X factor! It is difficult to pinpoint, but within thirty seconds of seeing a showreel/ performance we would know whether they have this. They would also have to be completely natural in front of the camera with the qualities previously mentioned.

What is Val's advice for those wanting to enter the industry?

❝ Be realistic. It is extremely difficult to break in to presenting, and they just have to be really lucky. If they do not get the job their agent may be able to give feedback in the form of constructive criticism and a presenter must be able to accept this, work on it and look forward to the next.

Wise Buddah Talent represents *Blue Peter*'s Andy Akinwolere, *Smart*'s Kirsten O'Brien, *The Gadget Show*'s Ortis Deley and BBC Radio 1's Greg James. What kinds of presenters does Wise Buddah take on?

66 Wise Buddah Talent represent a diverse range of dynamic presenters of all ages and varying expertise; however, we are very selective with our client list to ensure that we represent a roster of presenters who complement each other. Wise Buddah are a unique agency and have agents specialising in different areas including TV, radio, voice-overs, corporate and new media, so are able to offer talent an all-encompassing service. We look for presenters who are passionate about what they do and where they want to go in the industry, they must have a natural on-screen spark and a lust for life.

Angharad Marsh, TV Talent Manager, Wise Buddah Talent

## What a producer is looking for

You might have impressed the agent, but it's the producer who will be deciding whether you are hired or fired. Presenters can be selected by a commissioning editor, executive producer, series producer, producer or director. Unlike TV drama, casting agents are rarely involved. Producers usually play a key part in the process and having been given the brief for the series and the budget, they will look at the shortlist of showreels, and oversee screen tests and interviews. So what will impress the producers? Below, five established TV producers from different industry backgrounds give their expert opinion.

MAX GRAESSER  Formerly Director of Operations at ITV plc, has had a thirty-year career in commercial television, where he was previously Director of Production (Granada TV Productions) and Managing Editor of *This Morning*. He has worked with Gus Macdonald, Tony Wilson, Bob Greaves, Bob Smithies, John Huntley, Sheena McDonald, Lucy Meacock, Alastair Stewart, Richard and Judy, the original *This Morning* team – Chris Steele, Denise Robertson, Fred Talbot – and weather girls Becky Mantin and Chrissie Reidy.

Q  *What qualities do you look for in a TV presenter?*

A  The ability to think on their feet. The ability to remain calm in the face of adversity; that is, when things go wrong, and they always do. Intelligence – you want them to ask the questions you want asked and to come up with the ones you didn't think of. Grit in pursuit of an answer – many politicians and business people are trained to only answer the question they want to answer rather than the question they have been asked. Sensitivity – in order to ask personal questions in an acceptable manner. An engaging personality – after all, they are being invited into people's living rooms on a regular basis. A connection with the camera – the old cliché is true, the camera loves some people and not others, and there is very little you can do to change that.

Q  *What is the selection procedure, how do you find presenters?*

A  I have usually used presenters who are already known. Television is a very tough place to try out for the first time. Having said that, I have screen-tested presenters as a result of finding a moment of magic on an otherwise dull showreel.

Q  *What are the key elements that make a good piece to camera?*

A  Shape, clarity, fluidity, the ability to walk and talk at the same time – to show viewers what they are talking about rather than just tell them about it. After all, if you can't show viewers something you might as well be on radio.

Q  *What makes a good interviewer?*

A  Crucially, the ability to listen to what is really being said and if necessary abandon the original plan for the interview because something unexpected has just happened.

Q  *Is it easier now to become a TV presenter?*

A  More channels inevitably has lead not only to more presenting jobs but a far greater range and variety of styles. What hasn't changed is what makes a good presenter.

NIGEL DACRE  Currently Chief Executive of Inclusive Digital TV. Before launching Inclusive, Nigel worked with Ten Alps plc for five years, where he was the founder Chief Executive of Teachers TV and Managing Director of Ten Alps Digital. Previously he was the Editor of ITV News, in charge of *News at Ten* and the 24-hour ITN News Channel, Editor of the 1997 and 2001 General Election Results programmes, and the coverage of Princess Diana's funeral. Nigel was made a Fellow of the Royal Television Society in 2002. He has worked in the TV industry for thirty years, and worked with mainly the ITN and ITV News newscasters – including Trevor McDonald, Mark Austin, John Suchet, Dermot Murnaghan, Mary Nightingale, Kirsty Young, Nicholas Owen, Katie Derham, Alastair Stewart, Alastair Burnet, Julia Somerville and Carol Barnes.

Q  *What qualities do you look for in a TV presenter?*

A  When I was at ITV News, I was responsible for the ITV News presenting team. We had established newscasters, like Trevor McDonald, presenters from the reporters' team, like Mark Austin, and new talent from outside, like Katie Derham.

The aim was to get a balanced team – reflecting a range of ages and backgrounds.

They needed to have on-screen authority, an ability to deal with live broadcasting, and a background in journalism. But above all, they needed to develop a connection with the audience. I believe that viewers want to get their TV news from people they trust and believe, but also from people that they like.

Q *How did you go about selecting presenters?*

A I used to keep a careful eye on newscasters on other news programmes, other channels, and in the regions – and I would look at showreels sent in by individuals or agents.

Q *In your view, what makes a successful TV presenter? What skills and qualities should they possess?*

A The successful TV presenters are the ones who have the necessary qualities – on-screen authority or 'presence', an ability to handle live television, and the right experience. But they also need to be determined and focused. Becoming a presenter is not for the uncommitted or faint-hearted!

Q *What are the key elements that make a good piece to camera?*

A A clear, concise train of thought – and a presentation style that comes across as calm but interested.

Q *What makes a good interviewer?*

A As with newscasters, they need to have on-screen authority, an ability to deal with live television, and the right experience and training. But they also need to work hard in preparing for the interviews. They need to know the subject, and have carefully thought out the key areas of questioning.

Q *Do newsreaders have to be trained journalists?*

A The answer has to be yes, in my view – especially in the era of live twenty-four-hour news. A trained journalist will know about legal issues, such as contempt of court and libel. But also, I believe, that the viewer will soon pick up on a newsreader who doesn't have experience of news coverage.

ANTHONY GREENBANK    Has credits in the TV industry as Producer for Nuts TV, Producer/Director of *I Ran Off with My Toy Boy* (Sky), Assistant Producer of *RI:SE* (Channel 4), *Top of the Pops* (BBC), and Researcher for *Time Team* (Channel 4). He has been in the TV industry for over ten years and worked with Richard Bacon, Edith Bowman, Cat Deeley, George Lamb, Christine Bleakley and Olivia Lee.

Q    *What qualities do you look for in a TV presenter?*

A    A good TV presenter should have a mix of professionalism and personality. They must be competent, intelligent and hardworking, while also being likeable enough for the viewers. Another crucial attribute is the ability to remain calm and controlled when things don't go to plan. If your live TV show goes wrong, you need your presenter to paper over the cracks and steer the programme back on course.

Q    *How do you go about selecting presenters?*

A    Ideally I like to use presenters I already know and can trust. When this is not possible, or indeed suitable, I seek recommendations from other producers, as you can learn a lot more about a presenter from someone who has worked with them for six months than by watching a five-minute showreel. Screen tests are also important as they give you a chance to assess a presenter's character, talent and ability to deal with pressure.

Q    *In your view, what makes a successful TV presenter?*

A    First and foremost, you must be able to do the basics well – Autocue, interviewing, pieces to camera, etc. Given the ferocious competition in TV presenting, you should also be prepared to go that extra mile, especially in the early stages of your career – be ready and willing to get your hands dirty and work long hours along with the rest of the production team. If you muck in and maintain a high level of professionalism, the chances are that you will not only be hired again, but also recommended for other jobs.

Q  *What are the key elements that make a good piece to camera?*

A  The best pieces to camera are delivered from memory, rather than from Autocue. You can lose a sense of intimacy when using Autocue as the presenter is naturally forced to focus on reading the script from a screen, whereas if the piece to camera is memorised, the focus is on delivering the script to the viewer – and in television, the viewer should always be the focus.

Q  *What makes a good interviewer?*

A  A good interviewer must be a good multitasker. They need to simultaneously think, talk, take direction and – crucially – listen. Often presenters become so pre-occupied with their list of questions during an interview, that they fail listen to their interviewee's answers, and as a result seem disengaged in the interview. The best interviewers are the ones that are able to turn a list of ten questions into a natural, flowing conversation.

JACKIE ANDREWS   Has been Series Producer for Brook Lapping Education, and Producer for *Shariah TV* (Channel 4), *Kilroy* (BBC1), *Saw This and Thought of You* (Living), *Open House with Gloria Hunniford* (Five) and *Hypotheticals* (BBC2). She has been in TV production for twenty years, and worked with Gloria Hunniford, Clive Anderson, Kirsty Young, David Frost, Lorraine Kelly, Robert Kilroy-Silk, Paul Ross, Claire Sweeney, Alastair Stewart and Hermione Cockburn.

Q  *What qualities do you look for in a TV presenter?*

A  Professionalism, intelligence, someone who is comfortable in front of the camera and has an appropriate personality for the production. Easy to work with in a collaborative environment. Politeness – someone who doesn't mistreat junior members of the team. Not prone to outrageous demands. Someone who does their homework, can take direction but offer suggestions. The best presenters I have worked with are those who recognise that they are part of a team and that their contribution is often the tip of the iceberg. The worst have been those who believe their own hype and become difficult to work with. I know of one high-profile presenter who, on-screen, would have been perfect for a fairly major project I was working on, but the presenter was so difficult to work with that I told the series producer I wouldn't work with him. He wasn't considered for the job.

Q *In your view, what makes a successful TV presenter?*

A They need an intelligence, charisma, personality and certain authority on-screen. In a live broadcast situation they need to be able to quickly think on their feet whilst appearing unruffled. The ability to work with talkback.

Q *What are the key elements that make a good piece to camera?*

A Clarity, good pacing, varied and appropriate intonation. Depending on what the subject matter is, a certain stillness – both physical and emotional – helps so as not to distract from the content. Depending on the piece, an air of impartiality yet a projection of personality.

Q *What makes a good interviewer?*

A Someone who puts the interviewee at ease, asks clear questions, can listen to talkback without looking distracted. Someone who doesn't decide to follow a line of questioning that overtly reflects their personal views once the interview structure has been agreed between producer and presenter.

DAVID CHIDGEY    Producer/Director of *What If?* (Teachers TV), *Greatest Goals Against Man Utd* (Sky One), *Get Your Act Together with Harvey Goldsmith* (Channel 4), *Ricky Tomlinson Laughter Show, England: The Champions' Challenge* and *Sweet Chariot II* (ITV). David has twenty-two years' experience in the TV industry and has worked with Ted Wragg, James Nesbitt, Sam Delaney, Geoff Norcott, Dave Vitty, Jason Cundy and Jemma Keys.

Q  *What qualities do you look for in a TV presenter?*

A  A personality that connects with and engages the target audience; the ability to think on their feet; authenticity and credibility; someone who the audience can identify with or respect; the ability to take direction, especially through an earpiece; the ability to read an Autocue and to hit the mark visually and to time; knowing when the programme requires being witty, humorous and having the right look is also important.

Q  *How do you choose presenters?*

A  I generally use presenters I know, have worked with before or I've seen on other programmes. I will nearly always run a casting session or screen test before final selection just to make sure I haven't missed anyone who might be good. If completely stuck, I'll ask colleagues for suggestions and contact agents for reels.

Q  *In your view, what makes a successful TV presenter?*

A  The single most important point for me is their ability to deliver the material with authenticity and in a way that most effectively engages with the audience. Beyond that, looks, personality, technical proficiency are also important.

Q  *What are the key elements that make a good piece to camera?*

A  Relaying the material in an informative, entertaining and easily understood manner, being believable, authentic, and engaging. I want to feel that they are talking directly to me. Being authoritative.

Q *What makes a good interviewer?*

A  The ability to listen! Making definitive eye contact with the interviewee. Having empathy with what they are saying. An ability to coax more out of the subject than they are perhaps willing to offer. Being able to direct the subject down the correct path to suit the narrative and the editorial requirements of the programme.

## How to be a one-take wonder

Are you a presenter who can successfully deliver what is required in one take, or do you need five, ten, fifteen takes or more? If you are poor at performing, then you might find yourself replaced with a presenter who is more reliable and efficient.

Why? Time is money in television, so you just have to think how much time and money is being spent while you try to get the words out in the right order.

Failing to deliver has repercussions: some crew can be paid by the hour or by the day; the shoot may over-run; the crew will get tired and irritated; the director may not get through the shot list for the day; more material is being recorded, which will take time to check through and load into the editing system. So, more recording time and more editing time are needed if you are not able to remember your lines, or, if through nerves, lack of preparation or poor concentration, you make mistakes.

On the other hand, if you can become known as a 'one-take wonder', you will be popular with the crew, as well as the producer and production manager who control the budget, so you could find yourself booked time and time again. Preparation and professionalism pay off. Two or three takes are acceptable. If you need four takes the crew might start to get frustrated, and if you usually need five or more – read on.

Imagine a fairly typical scenario where a presenter has been hired for a one-day shoot to record all the pieces to camera for an educational series on classroom resources. Each of the six programmes in the series has an opening piece to camera, one in the middle of the programme and one at the end – so eighteen pieces in total to be shot in one day. It is common practice in television to shoot all the pieces to camera together as the presenter may be expensive or unavailable for longer.

To add good production value to the day, a top lighting and camera operator, and make-up artist have been booked for the shoot. The director decides to give the pieces to camera an interesting location, makes sure a highly experienced sound recordist is hired so that the day goes smoothly, and a runner is allocated to oversee locations, parking and lunch. As you can see, the costs are mounting up for what is a simple shoot with just one camera and one presenter.

The director is under pressure to get the recording and editing done as per the production schedule, because there is a viewing booked at the end of the week with the commissioning editor, who needs to see a rough cut of the complete programmes.

So the heat is on, and there are deadlines to meet. Of course, the director does not want to burden the presenter with these concerns as the presenter's job is hard enough.

A prompting device has not been booked as there will be several changes of location during the day and it would be time-consuming to rig, so the presenter will need to deliver the pieces to camera from memory. Scripts are sent out in advance for the presenter to learn. The expectation is that the presenter will have learnt at least the first few pieces to camera, and be very familiar with the rest, which can be memorised during the day of the shoot.

I was producer/director on a very similar scenario to this one. It was a shoot for Teachers TV and the locations were in Canary Wharf, London. We had to shoot eighteen pieces to camera, and chose several different locations in the area, each with a different backdrop. For each programme, the presenter had a costume change, new hairstyle and make-up, which had to be factored in to the day's schedule.

There was a heatwave so hot that we used umbrellas to shade us in between takes. Car parking was a problem throughout the day, and we had to keep an eye on the car and the kit. Parking permits were required in advance and there was tight security in the area. There were crowds of passers-by, problems with radio-mic interference and the sun was casting strong shadows on the presenter, who was also trying her best not to squint in the bright light.

For every piece to camera we did a quick rehearsal to check words, framing and sound, and then we went for a take. Usually the first take was good, but we did a second one for luck, just in case of technical problems in the edit. Each time we changed location it involved packing up the kit, and driving on to the next area of Canary Wharf, which took time. Changing costume, hairstyle and reapplying make-up was not straightforward as we did not have a truck for that purpose – we had to improvise on the day, making use of places such as cafés and toilets.

How did it go? Thanks to the professionalism of the crew and the presenter, we recorded all eighteen pieces to camera in the day. How did the presenter do it? By being prepared. If a presenter is totally reliable, the director can have more creativity and fun, taking risks without worrying if the presenter is going to fail. We recorded one memorable piece to camera as a boat sailed by in the back of shot – it looked fantastic. This was not a lucky chance, it was planned. Boats only came by every fifteen minutes, so we briefed the presenter that we would give a cue to start when the next boat was just out of shot. It worked perfectly and the presenter delivered a flawless take as the boat glided through frame. If the presenter had not given a good take we would have had a fifteen-minute wait for the next boat, – or, more probably, abandoned the idea.

As a director, I always appreciate it when a presenter gives me something to edit. In other words, rather than several half-finished takes, it is preferable to have a take that goes all the way to the end, even if it is not word perfect. You may have rearranged some words by mistake, but if the take makes sense it could still be useable. I suggest that you make every effort to get through the piece to camera to the end, even if you make some slips on the way; if the director wants you to do it again they will say so. It is possible that the director may be so short of time there will not be time to do a retake, but if you have given something useable at least the programme can be edited together.

Sometimes retakes are necessary, and are not the fault of the presenter. You might deliver a perfect piece to camera which is not useable because of interference on the radio-mic, or a camera problem. When on location there are numerous reasons for needing a retake, such as airplane noise or a passer-by in shot waving at the camera. The important point to remember is to redeliver your piece to camera as if for the first time. Make each subsequent take as fresh as the original one.

# PART FIVE

# Top Tips
# and Troubleshooting

All the exercises in this book can be done at home. You will need a mirror, preferably a video camera, some objects to demonstrate, a stopwatch, a friend to give honest opinion, to act as interviewee and give you timings; internet access would be extremely useful. Here is a quick checklist of some of the topics mentioned in the preceding chapters for you to practise.

- Recognise tension; relaxation techniques; deep breathing; breath-control exercises.
- Practise good posture, good eyeline; do physical warm-ups.
- Practise vocal clarity; read tongue-twisters.
- Scrutinise your wardrobe, accessories and personal grooming; practise smiling.
- Rehearse talking to camera on a variety of topics; keep a video diary; play back the recordings and analyse.
- Practise ad libbing.
- Practise talking to time.
- Research and write scripts and links, memorise them; start with short links and progress to longer ones, noting how long it takes you to memorise them.
- Practise talking while receiving instructions.
- Try out different genres; 'sell' products; create children's makes.
- Walking and talking – try delivering a script while walking; try walking and talking at different speeds.

- Practise interviewing a guest.
- Practise reading out loud, as if from a prompt.
- Watch television; study presenters; attend studio recordings.
- Focus on what makes you different.
- Research presenter-training courses and showreel production.
- Start shooting pieces; borrow or buy a video camera and editing software.
- Create your showreel.
- Create your CV.
- Self-promotion – create your own website; join presenter sites.
- Research agencies for representation.
- Look for job adverts and work experience on the internet and in the trade press.
- Make industry contact lists of production companies and individuals to approach.
- Apply for auditions.
- Top up your training.

*Some top tips from presenters*

**66** I would encourage anyone aspiring to be a presenter to also think outside of mainstream TV. I now present a travel diary on Sky.com and although this isn't television, the website gets over twenty million hits a month, something many lesser-known TV channels would love to be able to say. It has also helped to get me noticed by producers looking for someone with a reasonable amount of experience and been invaluable in teaching me how to write, produce and edit my own short programmes.

Lisa Francesca Nand, presenter, talkSPORT radio, Sky Travel; guest presenter, *Sky News*; journalist

❝ Have a USP (unique selling point), whether it is specialist subject or unique style or personality – to be different but ultimately to be yourself. Write ideas for shows, pitch them, be proactive. Get involved as much as possible in the industry, get experience, be professional and be personable to people you work with. Work hard with commitment and passion. On a couple of occasions I have presented jewellery on a web shopping channel. Not being a fan of jewellery and with no product knowledge, it was difficult to sustain any authentic passion over a period of time. You have to know yourself and work on things where you have a passion. Don't try and be all things to all people.

Howard Corlett, winner, *Sky Search for a Presenter*, 2006; presenter, *The Seven Wonders of the Weald* (Sky)

Presenting is a profession, so be professional. As you work your way through the top tips to practise, refer to the troubleshooting guide that follows.

## Top tips for troubleshooting and self-assessment

| | |
|---|---|
| I don't look at ease in front of the camera | Keep practising, especially relaxation and warm-ups. The more you present to camera the easier it gets. Remember to smile. |
| My voice sounds dull | Practise reading aloud, underlining the key words and phrases in each sentence to help give variety and emphasis. Talk with enthusiasm on a subject that excites you. |
| My diction isn't clear | Read tongue-twisters aloud to help form words clearly. Practise vocal training exercises. |
| I look like a rabbit caught in headlights | You need to relax. Do facial warm-up exercises, deep-breathing exercises and smile more when speaking. |
| What I'm speaking about isn't interesting | Know your subject thoroughly, speak with expression and passion. Practise speaking about subjects you are excited about. |

| | |
|---|---|
| My head is moving about too much | Remember the TV frame – small movements can look exaggerated on camera. A newsreader hardly moves his or her head but still gets the message across by means of vocal intonation. |
| My vocabulary is repetitive | Do you describe everything as 'great' or 'fantastic'? Find ten alternatives to make your scripts and speech more interesting. |
| I don't seem to be looking at the camera | Practise good posture. If your head is tilted too far back and you are looking down your nose at the camera, it can come across as distant and snooty. Look at the centre of the lens. Keep facing the camera – this is not a photo shoot, where you have a 'best side'. You must look straight at the viewer. Get your eyes tested – if you have a dominant eye, you may need to retrain yourself to be 'square-on' and not talk with your face slightly to one side. |
| I am talking too quickly | Usually this is down to nerves: practise relaxation techniques and breathing. Allow the viewer to keep up with your speech – a comma means 'pause', a full stop means 'stop'. Remember the general rule – three words per second. |
| I keep saying 'ums' and 'ers' | Try slowing down your rate of speech to give your brain a chance to think of the next thing to say. |
| I am not making sense | Structure what you are talking about; give your scripts a beginning, middle and end. Don't ramble. |
| How will I know how I am progressing? | As you progress through the exercises, try the harder tasks until you can do them all with ease. You will eventually receive feedback from the industry as you apply for jobs, submit showreels and attend auditions. See sections on how to find a presenting job, showreels and auditions. |

# Epilogue

## The professionals speak...

Hopefully now you have reached this stage of the book you will be inspired to give presenting a go! Presenting can be glamorous, exciting and an interesting lifestyle; perhaps some of the anecdotes will have whetted your appetite and given you the confidence to try TV presenting for yourself.

These presenters describe the benefits and highlights of their presenting careers so far:

**66** It sounds really corny but nothing makes me feel as alive as presenting. Even the preparation really fires my imagination. I never understood how it felt to be ambitious before! I think I'm addicted to the adrenaline as much as anything, but I also love communicating with people. I also like feeling like I'm good at something, without wanting to sound boastful – I get good feedback and that's very satisfying.

Cate Conway, presenter, *The Seven Thirty Show* (UTV),
*Cooking in the Community* (Northern Visions)

**66** I love interviewing celebs and you see that they are just real people like us! Some have even said that they are nervous or excited to be interviewed. Joanna Lumley was lovely and Sean Hughes was great too. I think the most exciting thing is everything I have filmed for veggievision.tv, because it's for my own business and something I really believe in too – which just has such meaning for me.

Karin Ridgers, founder/presenter, veggievision.tv

**66** I hosted a live corporate launch event at a prestigious venue involving celebrity chefs. The event was being filmed. With a short rehearsal period and last-minute changes, the concept involved running a game show. With a lot of specific information to convey and pressure to keep the show alive, it was exciting to deliver.

Howard Corlett, winner, *Sky Search for a Presenter*, 2006; presenter, *The Seven Wonders of the Weald* (Sky)

**"** The most exciting programme I have presented so far was a slot as a property expert for Channel Five. I was so excited as it's a huge channel, I am passionate about the subject matter, and also I used to watch the programme.

Charlie Lemmer, presenter, Real Estate Channel, Dubai Eye, Abu Dhabi TV, Current TV

**"** I presented a culinary festival in different locations every week for ten weeks. It was a lot of fun having very little script, mostly links and intros, and talking to the different cooks about what they were doing, because their personalities and dishes were each different. Plus it was outdoors! I really enjoy the spontaneity and variety and the opportunity to connect and communicate with individuals, as well as with a wide viewing audience.

Renée Castle, presenter, Caribbean New Media Group, Caribbean Communications Network, Sun Community Television

**"** I have a definite message that I want to share, and I see TV presenting as a means of being able to reach a much wider audience and make a greater impact in less time.

I really enjoy coming up with new ideas and conveying those to an audience clearly, succinctly, and in a way that captures and keeps people's attention – even when I am just in a studio essentially talking to a camera.

Marilyn Devonish, presenter, *The Life Success Show* (Sky)

**"** Interviewing Sarah Harding (Girls Aloud) was great as she is obviously a big name – I really enjoyed it because you realise that so many of these people are just normal and are really kind and helpful and actually quite nervous themselves!

Louise Houghton, presenter, sit-up channels and *SuperCasino*

**"** The most exciting programme I have presented is the Italian-jewellery slot on QVC, because I am passionate about jewellery. It's easier to sell when you genuinely love the pieces!

Denise Ching, guest presenter, QVC

**"** I presented a series of live web transmissions from a studio in Norway. This was a twenty-minute magazine programme each day for four days. We had guests for interview, musicians, taped inserts to make each day, all of which were based on events that were taking place the same or the previous day. The whole crew raised their game to make this work; that they only came together for the first time a few days before the first live transmission was amazing. That they represented four or five different nationalities was incredible. This was news-style production and broadcast. That anyone in the world could watch our activities live and interact with the studio (which they did) was very exciting.

Michael O'Donoghue, Higher Education producer/manager; presenter, Distance Learning TV

**"** I love talking and knowledge is very important to me. Knowing what makes people tick, and life itself, fascinates me. I'm interested in everything and TV presenting allows me to access a lot of knowledge and meet so many diverse people and visit many different places.

Charmaine Line, presenter, local-news.tv

# Appendices

## Resources

*Publications*
*The Stage*
*The Guardian*
*Broadcast*
*Televisual*
*Spotlight Presenters* – directory of presenters
*Contacts* – published by Spotlight, listing agents, photographers, TV contacts

*Online*
www.thestage.co.uk
www.guardian.co.uk
www.broadcastnow.co.uk
www.televisual.com
www.spotlight.com

*Websites for job searching, training, promotion and showreels*
www.talentcircle.org
www.mandy.com
www.bbc.co.uk/jobs
www.bbc.co.uk/newtalent/presenting
www.itvjobs.com
www.pact.co.uk
www.allauditions.co.uk
www.presenterpromotions.com
www.castweb.co.uk
www.startintv.com
www.castnet.co.uk
www.uk.castingcallpro.com
www.productionbase.co.uk
www.getpresenting.com

www.newpresenters.com
www.tvtalentsupermarket.com
www.shootingpeople.org
www.starnow.com
www.broadcastfreelancer.com
www.tobeseen.co.uk
www.pukkapresenting.co.uk
www.tellyfaces.com
www.presentersinc.co.uk
www.media-courses.com
www.radioandtelly.co.uk
www.pozitiv.com
www.screen-debut.com
www.skillset.org

*To train as a weather presenter*
www.metoffice.gov.uk
www.weatherschool.co.uk

*Courses*
www.actorscentre.co.uk
www.citylit.ac.uk
www.hotcourses.com
www.northernactorscentre.co.uk
www.ucas.ac.uk

*Training*
www.bjtc.org.uk (Journalism)
www.bbctraining.com (free online courses and glossary of terms)

*Books on voice*
*The Art of Voice Acting*, James R Alburger, Focal Press, 2007
*Voice and the Actor*, Cicely Berry, Wiley Publishing, 1973
*Finding Your Voice*, Barbara Houseman, Nick Hern Books, 2002

*To offer yourself as a guest interviewee*
www.findatvexpert.com

*To be a TV contestant*
www.itv.com/beontv

*To see examples of website presenting*
www.mywebpresenters.com
www.webvideos.co.uk
www.siteguidelive.com

*To order individually moulded earpieces for talkback*
www.nickway.co.uk

*Free prompting practice on a computer*
www.cueprompter.com

*Free audience tickets to see television recordings – watch professional presenters at work*
www.applausestore.com
www.sroaudiences.com
www.bbc.co.uk/tickets
www.pinewoodaudiences.com
www.beonlive.com
www.tvrecordings.com

*The Society of Teachers of the Alexander Technique*
www.stat.org.uk/index.htm

*Pilates Foundation*
www.pilatesfoundation.com/newsite/index.php

*Tongue-twisters*
www.thinks.com/words/tonguetwisters.htm

*To research production companies*
www.kftv.com (Kemps)
www.theproductionguide.co.uk (The Production Guide)

## Short, timed scripts

You can use these to memorise and practise with:

- ☐ 'Tomorrow we'll be showing you how to cook this delicious rhubarb and apple crumble made with the apples we picked earlier, served with a warm, vanilla custard. Join us then.' (*30 words, about 10 seconds*)

- ☐ 'Charities like this really do make a difference, not just to the children who are affected by this debilitating disease, but to their families. If you can donate anything, no matter how small, your donation will help to bring a smile to their faces. Thanks.' (*45 words, about 15 seconds*)

- ☐ 'School summer holidays – love them or hate them – will be starting for most schools in just under two weeks. In Monday's programme we'll be bringing you the definitive survival guide – how to entertain the kids on a budget, plan hassle-free away-days, and get through the six weeks without family feuds. Have a good weekend, and see you then. Bye.' (*60 words, about 20 seconds*)

- ☐ 'What is the secret of a successful barbecue? Preparation is the key. Before the guests arrive, marinate the meat, chop the veggies and salad, and have everything you need to hand, so that you can concentrate on getting the barbecue to the right temperature, and avoid undercooking or burning the food. I make sure the barbecue grill is cleaned of all old food, and place the charcoal under the grill, like so, no too closely packed. I use a very small amount of fire-lighter just to get the flame going.' (*90 words, about 30 seconds*)

- ☐ 'This woodland walk is one of my favourites. Further down it passes by a charming, babbling brook to the west, and in spring the area is completely covered in bluebells. These silver birch trees literally glisten in the sunlight with their almost luminous white-silver peeling bark, and on a crisp autumn day, like today, they seem to light up the path. I particularly love the wild, naturally growing ferns and hostas competing for my attention with their dark and contrasting leaf shapes, and here and there you can see cyclamen nestling in the undergrowth, with their shades of pink just peeping through. It really is beautiful here, and I can't think of better way to spend a relaxing Sunday afternoon.' (*120 words, about 40 seconds*)

☐ 'And so here we are on the marina at Puerto Banus, Southern Spain. This is the playground of the rich and famous – the King of Spain, King Carlos, moors his yacht here, as do the visiting celebrities and millionaires. Along the marina front you will find your very own little Bond Street, and if you are looking for that special Armani suit, Gucci watch, Rolex or Patek Philippe – this is the place.

You could while away the day in stylish restaurants or coffee bars, and there is plenty of glamorous nightlife too, where you might rub shoulders with regulars Melanie Griffith, Antonio Banderas, Kevin Costner, Elizabeth Hurley or Sylvester Stallone.

You can be pampered on the beach, or take part in more sporting activities – you can hire a yacht, go paragliding, scuba diving, or visit some of the thirty golf courses on the sunshine coast.

The world-famous Los Flamingos golf resort is just seven kilometres from here, and it boasts four championship golf courses, plus the Ritz Carlton Hotel, famous for its spa, impeccable service and luxurious gardens.' (*180 words, about one minute*)

## Self-Assessment Checklist
## Talking to a Camera

| | YES | NO | NOT SURE |
|---|---|---|---|
| Do I look tense? | | | |
| Do I look relaxed? | | | |
| Is my posture poor? | | | |
| Is my posture good? | | | |
| Am I breathing from my chest? | | | |
| Am I breathing deeply? | | | |
| Do I look too serious? | | | |
| Do I look happy? | | | |
| Am I making odd expressions? | | | |
| Am I looking around the room? | | | |
| Is my eyeline to camera? | | | |
| Am I really talking to the viewer? | | | |
| Am I talking in a conversational manner? | | | |
| Are my facial expressions too large for the small screen? | | | |
| Am I moving my arms and hands too much in shot? | | | |
| Is my diction poor? | | | |
| Is my speech clear, with good modulation? | | | |
| Am I speaking too quickly? | | | |
| Am I speaking too slowly? | | | |
| Am I smiling naturally? | | | |
| Do I look confident? | | | |
| Do I look warm and sincere? | | | |
| Do I look well-groomed and neat? | | | |
| Are my clothes flattering and appropriate? | | | |
| Is my topic boring? | | | |
| Am I being interesting? | | | |
| Am I making sense? | | | |
| Is my script well-structured? | | | |
| Would I watch this presenter or reach for the remote? | | | |

## Self-Assessment Checklist
### Reading from a Prompt

| | YES | NO | NOT SURE |
|---|---|---|---|
| Is my face frozen? | | | |
| Do I look relaxed? | | | |
| Do my eyes look glazed over? | | | |
| Do I have good eye contact with the viewer? | | | |
| Am I reading to the viewer? | | | |
| Am I talking to the viewer? | | | |
| Is my facial expression appropriate for the subject matter? | | | |
| Am I reading to the end of the sentence? | | | |
| Am I reading in short phrases? | | | |
| Am I running out of breath? | | | |
| Am I reading too fast? | | | |
| Do I have a conversational tone? | | | |
| Is my diction poor? | | | |
| Is my speech clear, with good modulation? | | | |
| Am I reading accurately? | | | |
| Have I mispronounced words? | | | |
| Would I watch this presenter or reach for the remote? | | | |

# Acknowledgements

I'd like to thank the Actors Centre, City Lit, Ravensbourne College, the presenters I've trained and worked with over the years, and the University of Bedfordshire for supporting me and giving me so many opportunities to teach TV presenting.

My sincere thanks to all the experts, colleagues and friends from several areas of TV production who have generously contributed to this book.

*Kathryn Wolfe*